MOM EGG REVIEW

2018 Vol. 16

Half-Shell Press
New York

Mom Egg Review is an annual collection of poetry, fiction, creative prose, and art by and about mothers and motherhood. *MER* promotes and celebrates the creative force of mother artists and sustains community through publications, performances, workshops, and online at www.momeggreview.com.

Front Cover Image: John Oliver Hodges

Mom Egg Review is a member of the Community of Literary Magazines and Presses.

This publication has been made possible, in part, by a grants program of the New York State Council on the Arts, a state arts agency, and the Community of Literary Magazines and Presses. *Mom Egg Review* is grateful for this generous support. *Mom Egg Review* is also grateful for the assistance of The Motherhood Foundation, and for the support of individual donors. With thanks to founding editor Alana Ruben Free and founding publishers, Joy Rose & Mamapalooza.

Mom Egg Review can be purchased directly from the press, through online retailers, at select independent bookstores, and through EBSCO. Contact *MER* at info@themomegg.com for info about discounts for quantity purchases and for classroom use.

ISBN-13: 978-0991510740 (Half-Shell Press)
ISBN-10: 0991510747

Mom Egg Review
Half-Shell Press
PO Box 9037
Bardonia, NY 10954

info@themomegg.com

www.momeggreview.com
www.facebook.com/themomegg
Twitter: @themomegg
Contact: info@themomegg.com

MOM EGG REVIEW

VOL. 16 - 2018

Editor-in-Chief
Marjorie Tesser

Poetry Editor
Jennifer Jean

Readers for Vol. 16
Jessie Bacho, Patrice Boyer Claeys, Becky Ellis, Elizabeth Lara, Jennifer Martelli,
Carole Mertz, Theta Pavis, Catherine Rockwood, Ana C.H. Silva, Judy Swann,
Melissa Thomas, Becky Tipper, Cindy Veach, Paulette Warren

EDITORS' NOTES

Marjorie Tesser
Editor-in-Chief

Welcome to *MER* Vol. 16. This issue was planned as a discussion of the ways in which mothers work and play, "play" and "work" being ways we characterize time spent; they are often considered a dichotomy, one or the other, heads or tails.

We had expected to get a fairly even distribution of submissions about work and play, but what we received was an wealth of poems, prose, and stories about mothers working and few about mothers at play.

This is not surprising, considering the many kinds of work that mothers do. For many of us, the choice is not work or play, but work or work or other work, with whichever "work" attended to often being done at the expense of equally crucial and necessary work. To go back to the coin analogy, it's clear that in most of our lives, not only are both sides of the coin fairly well occupied by work, there would be good arguments for including the rim. So where's the room for play?

As the writing in this issue reveals, whether an activity is considered play or work is more nuanced than a coin toss. While some jobs are onerous, tedious, or grueling, the doing of work, or a job well done, can also be a source of joy. And an activity deemed play, while enjoyable, often must be worked at.

Maybe play can be viewed as the coin's pleasure at being liberated from purse or pocket, at lofting, at the glint of light it reflects as it flies through the air. And at the arc's completion, its drop, or being caught.

As practitioners of mindfulness know, the act of giving your attention to a task elevates it. The works in this issue closely observe and show the nuances of work and play, as and for women, mothers, artists. Curating and assembling this issue has been a labor of love, both work and play at the most deeply satisfying level. Thanks to our contributors, to Poetry Editor Jennifer Jean and our dedicated and discerning group of readers for the issue, to all of our online editors and mostly to you, our *MER* community of readers.

Jennifer Jean
Poetry Editor

Most evenings my husband and I sit in our red living room and communicate via pop culture quotes. Our repertoire is limited to: *Star Trek* shows and movies, Jane Austen books and movies, *Star Wars* movies, *Lord of the Rings* books and movies, *Harry Potter* books and movies, and the odd *Casablanca* or *The Wedding Singer* quote thrown in. So, when I start talking about The State of the World, and What I Should Do About It via poetry and my writing life, he quotes fish-faced Admiral Ackbar from *The Return of the Jedi*: "IT'S A TRAP!" He is so wise (they both are).

This quote does double duty: 1) it reminds me not to forget to have fun (when I think of what I "should" do I often forget to have fun, and then what I end up doing—or writing—is often a joyless task, and as a resultant product, devoid of joy); as well, 2) this quote reminds me that fun, and joy, and play are also viable content in poetry.

At MER we will forever celebrate the work of mothers and, for this issue, received so many amazing poems about our work (which is too often under-celebrated). But I'm so grateful "play" was included alongside "work" as part of this year's theme. Play can be a powerful antidote to The (awful) State of the World (I don't say "act of resistance" because I'm with Carl Jung: "What you resist, persists."). So, in solidarity with my fellow MER writers doing the "work" of "play," I offer up this poem about the other kind of fun I have in the evenings at home:

Sweet Chariot

When I look at other men
looking at me, I think, *If*
you're not my husband
you're my brother. I hold my husband
in the near night.
The kids are away
in the red living room, a movie loud.
We've the ocean loud
too—spinning, like music.
Here, at the confluence of our mouths
we are electric, the opposite
of drowning. He is the one
that may bite my collar bone. &
I've hope he'll thrust home
with some exacting tilt—
till his *O, O, O,* as I
stroke, sounds of
Home, Home, Home—
till we are one so much
we are God.

CONTENTS

Cover Art: John Oliver Hodges

MOM EGG REVIEW

VOL. 16 - 2018

Elaine Terranova

Suckling

There I was, suckling a baby. It wasn't my baby for I never had one. I had the care of it from someone seated behind me, a big woman in a periwinkle coat. She said when she was away from the baby, her chest grew wet just with the thought of it. But she had to let it go now so she could get to work. The baby took to me right away. It rooted around like a pig and found my right nipple. It was a fat baby, a girl baby, skin just the color of my skin, so it blended and its flesh became a piece of my flesh. I felt the tiny mouth applied. I felt the warm stream of liquid draw through my breast. I wouldn't easily be able to separate again that baby from the rest of me if the mother wanted it back.

Margaret Young

Telemundo Univision

Nursing, shelling peas one-handed,
Arcade Fire's "Suburbs" turned up, telenovelas
on mute: *Duelo de Pasiones, Dos Amores de Ana.*

A man falls from a horse scared by a rattlesnake.
A woman staggers, hugely pregnant, across a footbridge.
The pigtailed girl pulls a knife on the man in the cowboy hat.

The lovers kiss in water to their waists.
The villainess is always blond.
The wounded man calls out for Emilio.

Cristin O'Keefe Aptowicz

Ramiro, Age One, Taconic Lake

Mama! Mama! You Italian film star you.
Giant blue eyes filling with tears on cue.
You are a jealous co-star to your big brother,
always wanting the meaty role he is playing,
always grabbing at every shiny award placed
in his tiny hands. *Mama! Mama!* You bleat,
neck strained, a perfect profile of unrestrained
anguish. But you haven't yet learned to handle
the fame. When you are put in the spotlight,
you blush, bury your head in a lap, look to see
what your brother is doing. Tonight, you didn't
want to go to sleep and your exhausted mother
happily passed you to my lap. *Mama! Mama!*
you wail as she leaves the room to cool down.
I use the only trick I know, whisper like I am
telling you a very important secret: *Listen. Listen.*
Mama is right over there but I need you to listen.
And finally you do, and I tell you about tomorrow,
the amazing day you'll have, about the lake, and
the fish, and the frogs. How you'll ride in a canoe
with Pop-Pop, and how Grammy is going to swim
with you, and you finally quiet, knit your eyebrows
together as you focus on my words. I tell you to rest,
your head on my chest, and to look at the lake, think
about all the wonderful things waiting for you
tomorrow, *tomorrow*, which will only happen
if you just close your eyes and go to sleep.
And you do.

Alexa Doran

My Son Watches Dolphins Die

amongst the faux coral and funnel
of fish eyes that pattern his night
light. Then waits while they resurrect
on the other side; a sort of nautical
parade between now and the afterlife.

He expects them to extinguish.

and return. Extinguish and
return. It's not that the painted
blue smiles and comma curved
bodies of these cartoon sea
creatures are Jesus backpacking
between death and life—
but the same interminable spirit is there.

We haven't talked about God

yet we have watched jellyfish
pout against the glass. We have
bought season passes to the butterfly
room. Who knows if they even noticed us?

Their whole world aflutter and my son trying to see
color, and then

seeing color fly.
Magenta lifted its wings and took off.
Violet clung to him.

Still it's not flight that pulls my son
to this circus ring of dolphins,

it's not weightlessness
that dangles like a rope
in a bell to be rung.

How could he choose what to celebrate?

The room glows
we are bent toward each other
two boats in a berth of blue gloom
one dimensional dolphins saunter by

two by two
two by two

Catherine Rockwood

As conservators build boxes

As conservators build boxes
to save what's rare
or worn, by time.

As wax is worked for loss
ceding to brass
or bronze.

As artisans'
minds worry at design
shaping it slant or slighted
punched or rubbed, so I

plot rooms for weary thylacines
tired hydras
and infants sleeping with pressed lips
like soaking, soft Möbius strips.

Penny Dearmin

Properties of Matter: Soft

How do I explain soft to a seven-year-old boy? Brady notices the bitter lemon scent of a new hand soap, the teeth of a table saw biting lumber ten streets over, the pulse of too many people in a room—the tension of sweat and breath. As an eighteen-month-old, my son had three words he rarely used: dada, baba, mama. He lost them all, even the word mama I thought he'd never say. The doctors softly murmured words about him that started small: autism; and got bigger as he did: autoimmune mediated neurological disease. I haven't been able to stop words from bobbing out of his head like water splashing from an overflowing barrel of apples; but, I have been able to bring him closer to understanding them each time.

In first grade, Brady's greatest challenge is writing beginning-middle-end stories; the very words that come closest to my love for him, separate us. Language isolates us even in science as I try to demonstrate the properties of matter. He spies a book and touches it without looking at me and I say, "No. It's hard, not soft. Soft is your pillow or a marshmallow."

He grabs a marshmallow and snuggles it against his face. He sees paper and scratches it across his no longer chubby cheeks. He lays the lined paper down and knows what it is not. Yet, he still does not know what soft is. Does he understand my love for him? It, too, is something you cannot see.

*

When I was seven, soft was the silky disk of pie dough rolled out from the force of my great grandma's strong arms and brisk ball-bearing-driven rolling pin. The flesh that hung from GG's arms was lenient like a pillow. I would nap in the cradle of her easy chair watching Sesame Street after slapping dominos on her round wooden table. Her fingers softly pressed the keys of my parent's piano as her brown orthotic shoes bent with each damp of the foot pedal. Her satiny, made-from-scratch butterscotch pudding soothed all my fears as she embodied the safety of maternal love. But I didn't strive to become more like her until my own children were born.

*

Soft is not how Brady appears to others. His firm grasp on humor is not always appreciated. He recently told his Grandpa, "Trees are nature's toilets. Everyone pees on them." His actions and beliefs are also not pliable or flexible. You cannot convince him that the failed 2004 poisoning of the Ukrainian President is anything other than a success story. As a nonfiction writer, I'm most proud of his sharp wit, which is anything but soft as he proclaims, "I'm not a liar, I'm just a terrible truth teller."

Brady's voice can sound harsh in a classroom of children when he blurts his answers. His touch is often rough as he crashes into people as he cannot sense where his body is in space. He squeezes my hand with desperation and talks too closely. His affection smothers me as he curls like an S around my entire body. His impact on me is not soft, subtle, or light.

The world is a shocking place for him to dwell. The smell of an orange can send him into a rage, as will the thought of being touched by someone who has eaten fruit without washing their hands. A chair scooted across the floor can halt his entrance through the door as he puts on his brakes and freezes. A typical childhood pastime of rolling down a grassy hill is like being stabbed while falling in a fire ant bed.

Soft is how I feel about Brady—raising him has transmuted my interactions with the world. From his first bath as a premature infant, when I cupped his small head entwined with a clear plastic oxygen tube above the royal blue plastic tub—my heart softened. My entire life I rejected being seen as soft towards anything. I was loud, passionate, and harsh in my beliefs. I thought being tough would protect me from the often cruel world. I have been proven wrong enough to know that accepting defeat can be seen as soft, but being destroyed is not in any way weakness. I softened out of necessity: for my survival, and my children's.

The seeping of my son's perspective into my words and the sifting of my words through his mind have shown me the interdependence of fighting to live, and writing to teach what cannot be seen, that mark my existence with him.

Soft is whispering a story to my son as he falls asleep, and staying up too late to read a book with squinted eyes and pressing keys to write and teach others as I go. Hard is missing the chance to do so.

Nancy Reddy

Travel Ghazal

We are in the Pennsylvania. Where is the turnpike?
Mama, where is our home, mama?

Look that truck. Look that big big dump truck.
The bicycle is on that car. You can hear me, mama?

Our car is blue. That cloud is upside down.
The sky is not made of water. Why, mama?

I can have a graham cracker? You can hear me?
I want to get out. I want to get out, mama.

Why not? Where is New Jersey?
The lady will tell us. The lady on the phone, mama.

Mama mama mama mama mama. Where is the broken car?
Where is our home? What's after home? What next?

Jennifer Stewart Fueston

Taking the Baby to See Rothko at the National Gallery

Fifteen minutes before closing seems like more time
than we'll need to see all there is to see of Rothko's
blocks of color, the hungry purples smeared on
canvases, the primal reds. The baby likes the moving
walkway, mobiles, flickering lights, the giant blueberry-
colored rooster crowing at the city from the roof.

I assume abstract expressionists will be a bit beyond
his comprehension, forgetting that they're art stripped
down to form, to line and color, to oval and ochre, to
rectangle and rose. So that when his babbles echo off
the surfaces in Rothko's room, I see he understands it
more than I will, pre-verbal, full of awe, himself another
masterpiece of bright, unsayable things.

Sherine Elise Gilmour

Sad Animals

Draw a sad rabbit you said.

And I did. This is what we used to do. Each night for weeks. Construction paper. Pink, yellow, blue. You would tell me what to draw and what to write, because you did not like the way the marker felt in your hand, pressed to your palm.

Draw a sad elephant. Draw a sad cow. Make him cry.
Draw a sad frog.
Draw a sad squirrel.

Draw a family of sad rabbits. Write "sad rabbit family." No no no, they're sad, they're sad. You cried and demanded when I tried to give an animal a smile. No no no. They're not happy, they're sad.

Nicelle Davis

Refrigerator Art I

I.   The drawing by Age 10 is this:

Her face, a fresh egg, looks out with noticeably different-sized eyes.
A dress, made from Magic Markers, has bled a bit in the construction

fibers—her body is something of a stain. A heart splits into a gaping
hole—his must be her mouth, for this is where a mouth would go.

Her neck is held in a crayoned vice. A giant razor-blade, dangles. Her
hair is stacked high as the drawn guillotine—layered yellow circle-curls

suggest something electric. A coffin-shaped man stands near, holding
a rope. His face is an unlit taper. His smile, a red liquorish horse shoe—

sweet and lucky. When I ask Lia what her picture is about, she says
the beginning of democracy, slice of cake—enough for everyone.

II.   Parental Response

Dear Age 10,

I was too impressed with how right you sound to say,
you're wrong. When Marry Antoinette told people to
eat, she meant she didn't understand the law of the land—
she didn't even have land; she was land to her husband
who was not a man but a metaphor for law. Few could
afford white bread, so bakers gave it freely—metaphor
against metaphor. When asked about freedom, Marry
replied she believed in sweetness—that if bread is free,
let it be free. Only bread is never free. They killed her
and so killed a metaphor and in doing so laws did morph.
The guillotine is the perfect metaphor—death hung from
a string—for we can cut puppet but the players always
remain. The beginning of democracy is not in the blade,
but in the giving of bread. Bread, remember, is never free.

Refrigerator Art II

I.   The drawing by Age 8 is this:

        Thirteen figures—some sticks, others with torsos fleshed to plump raisins, run about the 8 x 11 paper. Some spout interjections like "Run" spelt with a backwards N or "Fu…" "…it." There is, in fact, a bobbed-blond smiling

        from behind a box-shaped counter; she sells apples, bananas, grapes. Just behind her, a volcano is blooming. She looks satisfied, her concession-stand the perfect end-of-world business. Who wouldn't want a final taste? What is

        this? I ask Aria. Pompeii, she says. In the left hand corner, two line-thin people sit with a checker board between them. I ask her why the couple is not running. She explains, *they're old and are not afraid of dying.* Above is a mess of brown

        on top of blue scribbles. *They've been dying for so long*, she tells me. The sky indicates soon no one will be able to breathe. *They understand there's only time for one last…*

II.   Parental Response

        Dear Age 8,

        I'm too old and not young
        enough to play checkers.
        Does that make me the con-
        cession or blooming volcano?

Refrigerator Art III

I.   The drawing by Age 6 is this:

Stacked arches where red paint drips onto
a frantically brushed black sky. *A rainbow
at night,* he tells me. Titled: *The Universe.*

II.   Dear Age 6,

I won't tell you what can
or cannot exist, even if
allowing you to keep a U-
niverse requires being
monster instead of mother.

Katherine Barrrett Swett

Russian Doll

You sit on the nursery shelf
synecdoche of ancestry
and playful symbol of her self.

Though I don't play when by myself,
or violate your unity
as you sit on the nursery shelf,

my child unburies your smallest self,
the one that she has chosen to be
a playful symbol of herself.

She names the largest as yourself,
mother of unfolding fecundity,
who sits on the nursery shelf,

seven dolls from the tiny elf,
who by her childish metonymy
is a playful symbol of herself.

Or is that inner doll itself
the Eve of shrouding progeny,
while you who sit on the nursery shelf
are the playful symbol of herself?

Tara A. Elliott

Popsicles

After the foraging,
bits of fern, smooth stones, & pinecone safely tucked into basket,
mosquitoes collect at the napes of our necks, and we share Popsicles.
Yours a dark grape, and mine, bright tangerine.

Maryland humidity paints streaks in our own sweat, as it drips
down our dust-covered legs. At three, you only know how to lick the cold ice,
and your eyes open wide as I show you how to slide the icy juice up the stick to bite.

By the end of it all, you are coated in color, ants rejoice at our feet,
& as your sticky fingers hold both empty sticks—I freeze this into memory:
this all gone; this want for more.

Tamara Hart

A Prayer to the Mid-Morning Crow

It's hard to admit that the brain,
runs this whole (gestures around the room).
You want to be in charge of
the words on the screen,
the sex that feels good
down there, not up, limbically.
This man, this baby, this life
or knowing that crows are black.
But in this mid-morning light,
on this fence outside this house,
inside of which laundry and diapers
and dust balls and dishes are heads
of a domestic monster that grow back twice
for each you slay, this brain and its nodes
are telling you the crow is blue.
So blue you question its crowness.
Maybe Poe's opium-riddled brain
mistook a finch for a raven,
painted his brown frock black,
extended his beak, curled his feet,
turned his chirp into an ominous creek.
Crow, stay blue, like oceans in photographs.
Stave off these hands the brain puts to work—
laundry, diapers, dustballs, dishes—
Crow, stay the opposite of movement
blue the opposite of words,
never un-blue or whatever it is
I see through the window, in need of a wash.
If ravens can be finches,
this life can be more than this house,
this laundry, this diaper, these dishes,
this brain, this (gestures around the room).

Tatiana Forero Puerta

A Poem for All the Poems I'll Never Get to Read

I'm sorry: my child is a howling banshee
and all I want is to get through your next
stanza and maybe the last titillating couplet
eyeing me like a whiskey-sipping, six-pack cowboy
by the end of this lifetime.

But it doesn't look promising—my office is Noah's Ark,
though instead of animal pairs, it's flooded
with collections of other's sweat & sorrows
I'll never get to swim in.

There are sestinas that know me
better than I know myself and villanelles
that look me in the eye with that
wanna get outta here 3 a.m. look,
sonnets that might hit the spot
no lover yet has,

but I topple with each toddler tear
and paddle through an ocean of alphabets
to get to him even if he pulls me under and we bring
everything that has ever been written, all my long-
lost lovers, unread, right along with us.

Marian Brown St. Onge

Shoo fly

I, too, have closed the door on those I love with all my heart
—Closed it hard.

My children's eyes, bright and sharp as spices, would turn to moons
When I'd shoo them off.

"Shoo, Fly, Don't Bother Me!"—a song first published in 1869—has been recorded
on many children's records.

Katie Manning

Which Way Do You Want to Go?

I ask this question more than you might think, mustering my best Muppet voice every
time. And now my 4-year-old watches *Labyrinth* as I did at his age, and I am becoming
you: shuffling around the kitchen in the same style of open-toed house slippers that you
always wore, baking chocolate rolls or biscuits. *Yes, which way?* The blue hands insist
on an answer. Sometimes I look down at my hands and see yours kneading the dough.
I would choose this if I had a choice.

Claudia Van Gerven

Trying to Defect: For My Husband Vacuuming

> And if wedded, kill guilt in its tracks when we stack up the dishes
> And defect to the typewriter. - Carolyn Kiser, "Pro Femina"

The vacuum cleaner

makes its own tracks up the carpet nap.

You pull it by its neck

and it skitters after you—an ancient Eumenides.

You tell yourself you are not angry.

You tell yourself you are being kind.

You don't even know what a god you have by the throat.

I long to throw myself under its plastic wheels;

I feel the pull of guilt from its vacuous center.

No fatal scissors to cut the thread,

but no less chthonian for that—

your sucking machine

with its round mouth and it empty stomach,

swallowing up the graceful dust puffs

that danced under my bed at night,

and the mud oracles the dog tracked in.

Now it sniffs and pokes at my secrets,

trying to suck these words off the page.

Rebecca Hart Olander

Pressed Flowers

Rainer, you thought the heather I plucked
and sent your way, tucked in the sheets of a letter,
was not something I could see the beauty of,
and so you must tell it to me in your return post, make of it a Thing.
As if I were not the one with my face in the flowers,
tending our daughter without you, of whom you once said,
I believe that the only time I lived without loss
were the ten days after Ruth's birth,
when I found reality as indescribable,
down to its smallest details, as it surely always is.

This, to your own wife, left with our five-year-old girl,
my sculptures lumping half-formed in the corner,
a sink full of crusted bowls, the dirty linens piling up,
unable to take your advice and dedicate myself
to description. I smell death, too,
in the heather, bitter-edged
and steeped in tea and autumn.
You admit shame at not having noticed
the beauty while wading through it,
and my face falls reading your words.

Do you not remember that afternoon, the baby's cheeks
flushed with sleep while we made love right there in the heather?
This is what I meant to conjure for you:
the scent of home, of my earthy desire, and the way I made you wait
before entering me, buzzing bees an explosion in the purple cloud.
As always, you are in your own reverie, painting fissures
and fireworks out of flowers with your words,
everything your muse, save your Clara, and, for a little
over a week once, our daughter was enough
to dam your sorrow at the transience of the world.

J.C. Todd

Aubade

Dog-eared pages, penciled-in notes,
fuschia post-its tagging necessary
lines. The foolscap in ring binders

tea-stained. Two plates, crumb-rimmed,
a gummy shot glass. Some peels,
a core, old stems and seeds.

Up to that rubble of slow thought
and hunger, I climbed the narrow stairs,
jiggling this night's cup of something

hot, the hem of my fleece robe
a billow of fuzz collecting dust.
No street noise. No house noise. No heat.

It was bare-floored, cramped, a hermit's cell
of what I loved without reproach. To the
percussive of the keyboard, I wondered

alone, staring into the black moat
of airspace between stucco walls
where there was nothing to see except

what was in me, the findings of reading
and sorrow. When dawn pinked the room,
I came down, emptied, into

the rising light of my daughter's day.

Deborah Kahan Kolb

Emerging, Art of

Check the box that best describes
your career thus far, the form says, or how you see
yourself as a writer.

It seems I've been emerging
for a number of years now. But how do I see
myself - tunneling down the dark fleshy corridor
of my mother's cervix covered in ick, my slippery
soft skull bones mashed, intent on the drowning
sounds and the wreath of light ahead, finally emerging
to my first strident yawp?
And from that moment hence the steady
march of metamorphosis,
of emerging and becoming.

What must the torpid caterpillar do to emerge
from its glistening chrysalis a laurel-crowned monarch?
The worm digests itself. The lowly pupa
writes itself off in hopes of emerging
a butterfly laureate.
Self-immolation, it seems, is a requirement
for emerging.

So when you knock at the majestic doors, be prepared
for bleeding knuckles and a tamped
down spirit, be prepared to extinguish
yourself in a phoenix fire before you can emerge.
Established.

Susan Craig

Origami

I glide the steel iron
like a ship plying steam, press
napkins into perfect rectangles,
crisp triangles, squares;
I align patterned plaids,
flowers, birds,
colored edges, then

I lay them atop
linens hiding in cool depths
of their dining room drawer.
I walk by the table's dark wood
with its crackled turquoise vase,
one hydrangea faded to translucent
mauve over baby blue,
tinges of waning

green. From the dryer
I gather loose bundles of clothes,
hug the radiant heat to my
breast; snap out wrinkles
like firecrackers, old
matador flicking her cape—my
pulse clicks

like an igniting burner, then
subsides to the fine art of sorting.
One gray sock tucked in another
is a rabbit, the collar I starch
is hard white bone, bright
dotted boxers I invert
and whisk are billowing
kites that I

flick sharp as switches,
pat into contrite flattened packets.

24

Tomorrow they'll find them
in drawers like forever,
my touch disappeared—these
contortions, these
workings of my fingers,
all my dreams
folded neat.

Robyn Art

Zerrissenheit

Every few weeks we try to really get a grip on things, maybe get—like other, normal people—some of those giganto freezer bags of waffles, Bagel Bits, Hot Pockets; possibly brave the Kidz Gym, address the laundry situation, commandeer the grubby and chronically sleep-deprived offspring into the vessel while enduring the daily death march from hallway- to car-to place of employ; become, like the librarians planning a Little Mermaid-themed bridal shower, one of those Adult Disney Fans; like in the lifestyle magazines, unclutter the kids' rooms save for a few unaffordable wooden toys; cleaning up messes, crowdsourcing, crowdsourcing the cleaning up of messes, scrupulously stocking up on products which read "Compare To___;" at the Living History museum, buying the six-dollar-a-bag artisanal popcorn produced by autistic adults in a culturally-inclusive workshop; reading mom blogs and the fine print on the custody agreement; like a movie you keep waiting for it to be over. It keeps not being over.

*in German, "falling-to-pieces-hood."

Tina Kelley

The Hardest Day of My Four-Day Work Week

The grass looks scruffy, the wild onions growing taller,
the house unkempt as baby birds, messy as new mothers,
untamed as toddlers, newest things in need of a trim.
When you're in college this house will be neat.
And too empty.

The three of us play an existential version of Sorry!
She craves winning, he moves pieces randomly,
counting one five six three nine, infuriating her.

All day he makes his comic book sound,
a glottal peeeww, peeeww, peeeww over and over,
the sound of a punch and a bullet, as he upends the box
of a thousand crayons. He announces, "Mommy, you stinky,
you poop your diaper." When his sister approaches
he clenches in rage. She takes him down,
pushing hard against his heart.

What do you mean you don't like graham crackers?
How innocuous and sweet and fine can a food be?
That's like not liking the Easter Bunny.
Eat them. Now!

Please.

I try reading to them. The somnolent rhythms of the words work on me,
not on them, and I drift, chasing down what Seuss might have meant
with "I would not could not with a goat." Bad mommy!

"I cut your head off. I eat it for lunch," he says, and they must be starving,
it's after two. The day dances away from me, a tiny piece of shell
fished out of the egg white. "I drinky!" he hollers. She spills milk again.

Today I am a piñata, flailing, fragile, meant to fail,
beaten all day. Unnoticed, my gifts explode out and down.
I smell sunscreen and the outdoors in their hair.
They say they wish every day were Friday.

Carissa Stevens

Expatriate

They'd remodeled the break room.

This was to be expected, Tricia reminded herself. It had been years since her departure. Still, it jarred her—the stainless steel refrigerator, the clean tiled floor. Gone was the cracked microwave, the corkboard full of memos and post-it notes, the vending machine that sold stale Pop-Tarts and smooshed cinnamon rolls. She could remember sitting at a rickety card table and crying into her microwaved lunch. The card table was gone, too.

"Mommy," Henry said, "I thought we were going to the library." He stood on one leg, looking a bit like a flamingo.

"In a minute," Tricia said, hugging her purse. "Don't you want to see where Mommy used to work?"

"It's boring here," Henry said.

There was a soft thud as a man entered the break room clutching an empty coffee pot. He narrowed his eyes, studying Tricia. "Can I help you?" he asked.

"No," Tricia said. She felt her face warm. "I was just showing my son around. I used to work here."

"Is that right?" the man asked. He smiled at Henry.

"It is. I left six years ago."

"Off to greener pastures, I presume," the man said. He chuckled at his own joke.

"You could say that," Tricia said. "I needed to have…" The letters IVF nearly flew out of her mouth. She scolded herself; she now spent so little time in the company of adults that it was hard not to overshare. "I needed to take some time off. To have my son."

"I see," the man said. He averted his eyes and stepped over to an immaculate sink, filling the coffee pot with water.

"I hope no one will mind. Henry wanted to see my old office."

Henry groaned and smacked his hands over his face.

"I don't think anyone will care," the man said. He kept his gaze fixed on the coffee pot.

Tricia tugged Henry's arm. They walked into a large space full of cubicles and chatter. Water coolers gurgled, computer screens flashed. A harried looking man passed out bundles of mail. A woman stood, stretched, and readjusted her headset. Tricia was pleased to see her old friend Todd still occupying his cubicle—far right, near the window. She lifted her hand in a wave. Todd only blinked at her.

"It's neat in here, isn't it, Henry?"

"The library has sock puppets," Henry said.

They passed a large copy machine that was churning and beeping, collating and stapling. It smelled of toner: bitter, dirty, nostalgic.

"Look at that," Tricia said.

Henry huffed and rubbed the toe of his shoe into the carpet.

They at last approached a door with an opaque window, another name painted onto the pebbled glass. If Tricia squinted hard enough, she could still make out the cursive slant of her own name despite the silhouette of someone new inside the office. The figure's arms swayed as they typed.

She could remember the way it felt. The slick surface of a keyboard, the heft of a corded phone, the whirl of a rolodex, the cold metal of an ink pen tucked behind her ear. In her mind's eye, she could see a desk calendar full of hastily scribbled appointments and stacks of crisp, white paper that needed her signature.

Henry shook her arm.

"Why are your eyes closed?" he asked. "You can take a nap at the library."

Dara Herman Zierlein

Mary Pan

Back to Work

She wakes early, to her husband's alarm at 5 a.m. She lingers in the dark, the covers cocooning her. She opens her eyes, she closes them. It's her first day back to work after maternity leave. She spent the last four months with her three young children, nonstop in the summer sun. She's returning to that other work: the kind of work she's paid for, the kind of work she's trained for.

She falls out of bed and into the bathroom; it's still dark outside. Autumn has begun and rain falls, melancholy on the windowsills. It's comforting to her, fits her mood.

She creeps downstairs and eats a banana, heats up some egg white vegetable muffins. She's still trying to lose the baby weight. She distractedly does her devotional, poorly written by a Texan megachurch attendee, but the straightforward approach appeals to her religiosity; it's a solid start to the day.

She showers and dresses, her work clothes too tight or too loose in places, uncomfortable throughout. The baby stirs. She wakes her five-year-old daughter, who is sleeping in. She feels her forehead and speaks gently; her eldest had a fleeting fever last night. She doesn't feel warm but is sluggish getting out of bed. The girl heads downstairs to gather breakfast and get herself dressed; she's an independent first-born.

She scoops up the fussy baby, still swaddled, cheeks warm. She sits in the rocker recliner in the dark, nursing in her work clothes, foolishly hoping to avoid wayward spit up. The bedroom door is open just a sliver and she hears her three-year-old son stir next door. He jumps out of bed with a loud thud. His bedroom light turns on, turns off. She sees him emerge, hair tousled, his Christmas-themed pajamas askew. He yawns. He's adorable. He has two matchbox cars in hand. He looks this way, he looks that way. He doesn't notice his mother in the rocking chair, observing him. He scurries to the top of the stairs and listens.

Her eldest appears upstairs, fully dressed, to brush her hair in the bathroom. She can just make out her daughter's profile through the slit in the door, standing on the blue step stool, combing her hair just so, leaning forward over the sink to examine herself in the mirror. She looks to one side of her face, then to the other. The girl doesn't know she's being watched, regarded with wonder and sentimentality.

She rocks the baby in the recliner, back and forth, back and forth. The baby is done nursing but she can't bring herself to get up just yet. She snuggles the little one to her face, breathes in her baby's scent, her oldest daughter's self-scrutinizing, the sound of her son's matchbox cars moving on the hardwood floors. She puts the baby down in the crib as the nanny arrives at the front door. She moves out into the gray morning, carrying these images with her, in her weary but ready bones, as she rushes on to work.

Rebecca L'Bahy

Ode To My Commute On The Fitchburg Line

Because on the platform I can feel
bird song on my face.
Because alone with others is best,
all of us quiet, waiting—
for the eye that casts its light
upon the weedy track, anticipating
a blast of inexplicable wind
that smells like water left behind
after lobsters have been pulled
from the pot,
and the conductor's accent—
that's no parody of Boston's working class
but sounds like it should be:
Ay-ah Next! Ay-ah! comforts me.

Inside, where the horn's muffled blare
sings its one long note,
I slide in next to Walt Whitman,
happy to press my head
against the hard seat, give up time
and be where no one knows
or can find me.

Together in silence
we give praise to the world—
the tall grasses waving their feathered heads,

Thoreau's Walden in conversation with wind
and sky, followed by men
in hazmat suits, buildings marked
with misspelled graffiti
and someone's couch
abandoned in the trees.

It looks dry, inviting—
a nice place to sink
into a poem,
when later I sit
in my windowless cube.
In my mind's eye I see
the two of us there—
parentheses paused
under a canopy of trees,
our tongues heavy
and wordless as stones.

Jennifer Schomburg Kanke

Forgive Me, Discover Card Fraud Protection Work Station Twelve, 1989

Now that I know what a lunch break is,
to my mother I give a million thanks.
Drive us to the pool, or the library, or the mall.
Buy snacks, or stamps, pay the electric bill.
My endless list tacked on to hers,
chipping away at that precious hour
free from the gray maze of cubicles and headsets,
those few moments of rest eaten up
by teenage hungers while her sandwich
sat in its clear plastic baggie
forgotten in the break room fridge.

Jan La Perle

Rural Letter Carrier

Maybe the saddest thing is watching
my daughter stand on the edge
of the porch and call for
the neighborhood cat, watching her
from behind, her pajama bottoms
loose in the rump, and the cat
doesn't come. Or maybe
it's the dog wishing for a walk
when there won't be one, not a one,
because the husband is working
and I am working and I have more
work on top of that work
and my daughter's stocking feet
are jammed into her flip-flops
and I know she's crying now.
Or maybe the saddest thing
is when I go to the door with
a letter to sign for, and the lady
comes, and a face already sad turns sadder.
Once I had to step over a breathing hose
to get to a lady on a couch
and I couldn't see where the hose ended.
It stretched forever and maybe
it looked a lot like the road
in front of me and I know exactly
what is up ahead and I am scared.
One day I knocked on a door,
a package in my arms like a friend
I had been traveling with, and the man
on the other side said, *who is it?*
I didn't know what to say and maybe
that is the saddest thing. I am
the lady who likes your horses.
I am the lady who drove all day
to get here. I am the lady you'll
call in to complain about without once

looking into my eyes and noticing that
I, too, am waiting for the stray,
that I am watching my daughter
turn around after hollering, *Fluffy,*
again and again, the privet hedges
holding hands and throwing her little shouts
around the yard like all of this is just
a game to play and I am at the desk
with two computers on in a row.
Maybe behind the door with my package
I should have said I am a mother
who doesn't know what to do about
her daughter who is somewhere crying.
But people so often and almost always
miscommunicate, so you can imagine
what it is we are doing with the trees
and so often it is just me and them
on the road framed by the windows,
their branches hanging with their
little quiet bells of sadnesses
and my daughter's tears are like
raindrops on the window between us –
pretty and sad and not a single
thing I can do about any of them.

Anne MacNaughton

Vexation 23

I am
wiping the mildew from the bathroom ceiling
        when the phone rings / baby pees on my foot
                and briefcase spills / into coffee grounds.

Single moms do it all.

        I   CAN   EAT   FIVE   JOBS!

Sent off a check to the IRS
to pay for the bombing of Afghanistan.

I give it away.
        Some say if a woman sells it
she's cheap and low

say if she gives it away free
she's a fool.

Women do not translate well / into money.

E.J. Antonio

Washerwoman Dressed in Brown (as told by Indigo)

she stands apart from the frolics of soprano, alto, tenor, bass choir members and organ master. watch them collars and ties loosen. watch them skirts twist up and them buttons pop as the squirms and squeals of grown folks bathe the pews in sweat. y'all know how it is: one hem, one pair of suspenders always leaves with a second hand prize that's been passed around too many times. not my Esther. dressed in shades of oak and maple, she's there to clean for Sunday service. the sway of her long wool skirt brushes away the cobwebs clinging to the underside of pews. In the racks, bibles need dusting; pulpit lectern needs polishing; pine floors need scrubbing; cedar bathroom walls need scouring; linen chair covers need bleaching; reverend's robes need pressing. she works alone in a sanctuary full of church folk. no one offers to help. they are so preoccupied with needs of the body hidden under those choir robes. they ain't noticed, it's her beautiful work that shines brightest every Sunday, not their peacock singing.

Lorraine Currelley

Harlem Looks Like Apartheid (Domestics)

gentrification invades our eyes with its growing visual stench. our love putting food on our tables, cleaning invader's homes. it is our need we hear, when their children call us by our first names. we fold into ourselves, never dismissing this historical uncorrected violation.

diamonded mothers stroll casually, speaking on phones window shopping. while we domestics disguised as nannies push carriages with children old enough to walk. there is no equality in this poem, only constant reminders of ancestral enslavement, apartheid and their grandfather's Jim Crow. no neighbor, no friendship, nor equality, only their great great grandmother's generational handed down privilege, entitlement and beliefs of ownership. greed bleeding low wages and stolen labor.

it is love we breathe in deeply, each morning boarding buses and trains, preparing ourselves to clean Becky's filthy house. these markers reminders of classes divided by skin and memory. purpose brings us here, to these shores. promises of citizenship and always a better way of life. it is these promises, this seduction that temporarily cools the fires burning in our heads. our silence does not translate into docility and acceptance. we are both masters of this understood and agreed on generational deception, in this dance between the haves and have nots, women and opposing cultures. our smiling lies hide our revulsion, thoughts of our goals and freedom.

Angela Narciso Torres

What Binds

Sewing the elastic on my dance shoes
I think of Mary Lincoln sitting in her favorite
chair by a sunlit window mending socks
while her children played on the floor
in the yellow house in Springfield, Illinois,
where she made a home with the young
lawyer Abraham. I think of how sewing
is fast disappearing, though in middle school
it caused sweat to bead on my forehead
during Home Economics, mastering
the backstitch, whipstitch, chain-stitch,
the elusive French knot. As if perfecting
all the ways of fastening thread to cloth
would prepare us to conquer the world
of women. Or was the goal to bind us
to that world? Even the DMC thread we used
seemed shorthand for domestic. My aunt
once showed me a life-size cross-stitch
of an angel ascending to the heavens, each
fold in his white robes accented with silver-
gray. The project took her months to finish—
what helped her endure a rough patch
in her marriage. I wanted to study
her face as she told me this but by then
she'd already turned to her cooking.
Some schools believe working with hands
raises self-esteem in children. Making
a thing that wasn't before creates
a sense of agency. Today I sew
out of necessity—dance shoes
won't stay on without elastic.
I'm counting stitches, checking for
evenness as if planting seeds
in a plot. Why does it matter that
I hide the knots or pull the thread
just-so to keep the satin from puckering?

Meanwhile in a dusty factory a woman
drags a small needle through linen
so she can buy bread for her sons.
Elsewhere, a young man on a plane
knits his girlfriend a pink beanie,
endless loops linking him to knitters
through eternity. Deep in the night
of my closet lies a scrap of cloth
my son once sewed with the symbols
I <3 U. It came with a note—
Look, Mom, I made this for you.

Preeti Parikh

Garment

Neat folds, tucked in at the navel, fell in equal pleats to the ankles;
the free end, draped across the bosom, was pinned to the left shoulder—
thus, starch-stiff and creased, your off-white cotton saree wore itself
ceremoniously. You had come to meet with my teacher at school
(a role reversed from your own teaching job); I squirmed beside
you; your crisp saree folds brushed against my willowy arms.
The measured words you had whetted earlier now volleyed forth
at his wavering baritone. I twirled the edge of your saree around
my index finger; the voices trailed off. *Somewhere,* a woman bent
over a handloom mill hand picked each thread with care, crossed
the weft and warp with precision; the patterns crept in line by line.
The fabric exchanged hands, became *rupaya* and *paisa;*
meanwhile, her baby, cocooned in a sling carrier, dreamt reveries
in concert with its mother's moving torso molting into a newer woman.

eve packer

glitches & life or madame x and superkid

you know actresses really are like hookers,
in one way, only--we are not allowed to have
children--visible kids. its like one of those movie marquees
on 42nd: i was a Mutha, a secret Mutha, I hid my
Guilty Secret from the world—

oh i am so mad.
just lost an audition—
no babysitter.
the first piece i make (above, from memory)
i write on a paper napkin in a now gone diner
at 10 ave and 52nd:

that's the late '70's, and the old 42nd st—

Then: the spring of '81, i land at studio recherche, as an actress.
down those few steps, to the small blackbox theatre—
i am alice,
thru the looking glass, down the rabbit hole.
this is the developmental space initiated, run, mentored, by the great
mabou mines experimental theatre artists, ruth maleczech and lee breuer.
their mission: to take interpretative artists: actors, musicians, dancers, and
transform us into independent creators, performance artists who make our own stuff.
the catch: the only way to stay is to write your own work.
what can i do? i am hooked.

what to write about?
the only option, subject, i can think of: to create a piece about
the hardship unfair arduous impossibility of single mom/actress and child.
and to create it with my son. i do not want to exclude him the way
i feel my mother excluded me from her art. and then had to give it up
to support us.
And steady babysitting when you need it, for an audition, on the fly, at a moments
notice, impossible (without funds, and there are none).

children are welcome, part of the process, intrinsic.

i bring my son to the theatre and start to work. begin with a monologue.
he is in the bathroom—he comes out, and from behind goes into imitating me—
everyone flips. this is the start of the piece.

so, now: it is a two-person piece. my son, age 5, and me.
this is important: we improvise scenes; he improvises all his own words. i write them
down. we both memorize our lines.

we start work on our piece..
Since my son is 6, after the first 3 performances we put him on video (now converted
to dvd).

Recently I looked at the dvd: Our show:
i am reading to him, he kids around with answers to my questions.
a babysitting problem. I have an audition.
the babysitter cops out.
in filming, my son forgets his line. i keep feeding him the cue--louder & louder. he is
just about in tears, my voice harsh. we are both angry, hurt. this mirrors, is metaphor
for the whole problem. he remembers his line. we keep going.
a scene of me banging my head against the wall.
penultimate scene: he is in my arms; i am carrying him to the audition, we have our
coats on, and he is asleep on my shoulder.
last scene: at home, peaceful.

some of the lines he improvised:
when i'm reading to him: he says: NONONONO—you have it all wrong! very
playful, with his little action figures.
later: "how come i never get to go to an audition?"
it's not nice to be with somebody who's not yr parent all the time."
then: me: "i have to take you to this audition."

in performance, he wears
a thriftshop superman shirt, and i, as medea,
push him off the ledge: he jumps, and in the dark,
lands on a pillow. he loves that part.

early on i say to liza lorwin: i'm not a writer.
she says: now you are.

without my son i would not be a writer, of any kind.
my son is now a playwright.
from the start, he makes his own words.

IN looking at the video now, summer of '17: i am struck by the obvious:
my son is a grown man, and i, well, am an older woman.
and because of my son, i—evolved,certainly changed. i became a performance artist...
no auditions.
then, for economic reasons, took a full-time teaching position and after recherche
closed, became a poet/performer.
as a writer, you are, if nothing else, independent.
my son among other gifts, brought me that: once you are a writer you bring a
different approach to the words, the situation—you know, you can make your own
stuff.
because i have a son, and we made *glitches & life,* or *madame x and superkid*
together—we share that experience. and because of that experience and where it led,
i carry the flag that reads: independent artist.

This piece marks a turning point.
Because of this piece i became a writer.
and i became a writer because sam is my son.
long outgrown, are the clothes he wore.
my pants, now ripped, i still have, and the thermal top, striped scarf.
"time," as a friend says,
"is implacable." But I no longer bang my head against the wall.

Margie Shaheed

A Night at Mickey Finn's

"Girl, hurry up and get in here. The party is about to start and I need you on the floor! We had eighty-five people to RSVP, so it's going to be busy tonight—you had better put on your roller skates!"

Maria is the feisty manager of this popular strip club in downtown Cleveland. This proud Italian mama runs a tight ship. There's a long list of house rules she enforces, the first being *no illegal sex acts on the premises.* Hard talking and quick to put you in your place, underneath her brass-knuckle exterior is a softer side that mothers all of the girls who come from everywhere to perform on Mickey Finn's famous stage. I wait tables here on weeknights after I leave my day job at City Hall.

As I head to the dressing room, I bump into Heaven Lee, one of the regular strippers at the club.

"Maria says it's going to be busy tonight," I say, as I enter the room and begin pulling off my suit jacket and pants.

"I'm ready! Hey did you hear? The headliner comes from Arizona and she works with snakes," says Heaven Lee, pushing her face closer to the mirror to put on false eye lashes.

"Yeah, I've been waiting to catch her act. I hope I don't get too busy and miss her," I say, as I stick my arms through a little black dress and slide my feet into a pair of patent leather flats.

"Don't forget we're planning something special for Michael. Maria's got him a birthday cake. Of course, he'll buy the champagne. We'll sing "Happy Birthday" to him. He's such a good customer. I don't know what I'd do without him," says Heaven Lee.

"Don't worry, I've got you covered. I'll let you know when he arrives. Break a leg and I hope we make lots of tips tonight," I say, playfully.

By the time I hit the floor, the DJ has arrived. Men are filing into the club ordering pitchers of beer. Champagne is flowing. Music slices through air. Colored lights bouncing off the naked skin of go-go dancers make their glittery bodies look like eels swimming in an electrified pool. The party is in full swing.

I think about Michael as I prepare his special table. He isn't handsome; he's a bit of a misfit, with a penchant for thin brunettes. He likes Heaven Lee best. He lavishes her with gifts and always runs up a high tab for champagne, for which Heaven Lee and I receive hefty commissions. Michael is friendly, but has sad eyes like he's worried about something. We tease that he has a wife and children he doesn't care for properly at home. But our business is to create fantasy and play; there's no room for reality, so none of us, especially Heaven Lee, ever considered it seriously. I check my watch. Michael is late.

Zsa Zsa the Snake Woman brought the house down when she ended the night with a tantalizing belly dance. Her flowing red hair held a crown of black feathers and crystal beads. She mesmerized the audience with tricks she did with snakes that, from time to time, adorned her body like exotic pieces of jewelry. The men went crazy. They kept throwing dollar bills on stage, and the more daring of them touched her by putting dollars in her costume.

"Last call for alcohol," Maria shouted. Security had no trouble clearing out the club.

"I wonder why Michael didn't come tonight. We can put up his cake for him. Maybe he'll make it tomorrow," Maria said, as she began counting the night's receipts.

I was standing behind the bar washing glasses and listening to the local midnight news, when I happened to look up at the TV screen and caught Michael's sad eyes peering out at me from the camera.

"Maria, look, it's Michael. He's on TV," I shouted.

"Shhh, let me hear what they're saying."

"Go get Heaven Lee. She needs to hear this," Maria said, concerned.

It was a mug shot. Michael had been arrested for stealing money from a church where he was a longstanding member and treasurer. According to church officials, they suspect the thefts may have been going on for several years. When they became suspicious, they arranged a sting operation with local authorities, who caught Michael red-handed on hidden camera stealing church funds.

"Well, I'll be damned. That's why he could tip so well and buy champagne so freely. Now my good thing is cut off," said Heaven Lee, regretfully.

"But that was God's money!" said Maria, laughing.

"Humph, not while I was spending it. It was my money," said Heaven Lee, picking up her bag to leave.

"Can I get an escort to my car?" she called out to one of the security guards. It appeared she was pissed.

I didn't know what to say. But the two things this night did showed me was, you never know where your blessings are coming from, or when they will dry up.

44

Laura Ajayi

Michael Levan

Progesterone #2-22

With all that she must endure, still she hates most / the twice-weekly shots. The man does what he can to avoid / disinfecting the area too close to an old injection site, the black-and-blue / letting him know she's right about feeling *like she's been kicked in the butt,* / but there's only so much new room away from her hip bone / to aim the needle after his *Ready, one, two, three,* / such small space to shoot for that won't nick a vessel / and leave him scrambling for tissue or towel as the thin red line / follows her curve and down the back of her thigh / before he can blanket needle's exit in bandage, sheer adhesive or, if he's feeling cheeky, / one of the boy's Iron Man or Incredible Hulk Band-Aids. / Only so much time to examine for a new injection site when she cannot stand / for more than a few moments without want / to collapse, the two minutes he must slowly push / the Progesterone already a trial in endurance. He assures her / this also is worth a few moments' pain, but how can she trust him, / how can she let him speak their hope when he's had / so much less to suffer, so many more ways to escape, so much / more light to his days and nights?

Cheryl Klein

Future Perfect Tense

You are 24, a full-time student and full-time employee of the early Internet. You have never paid a bill late. You have never told anyone to fuck off. Your mom is going through treatment for ovarian cancer, so you send her a postcard every day, call every night, visit every weekend.

Although you worry a lot that you will never find a mate, you take it for granted that someday you'll have kids. You collect names, and not just because you write fiction. You think about the perfect Bohemian household you will lead someday, a cross between *Rent* and a Norman Rockwell painting.

You've worked since you were fourteen. Your father started a paper route at eleven. There are no Puritans in your family, but work is its own religion. Nine to five and then all the household things. Dusting and ironing and weeding. Your parents don't even own an automatic garage door opener.

Becoming a mother when you're married to a woman must also just be a matter of work. You assume so as a newly out 24-year-old and, still, as a 33-year-old with a troublesome fallopian tube. It must be a matter of monitoring and injecting and eating the right vegetables.

This belief will continue through three unsuccessful IUI's (that's a glorified turkey baster, dear uninitiated 24-year-old) and one successful IVF treatment.

You will be a pregnant woman for nine weeks. When you see a woman with a round six-month belly at a crowded In N Out on a road trip, you will give your seat to her, and then cry. Because she is a real pregnant woman, and you are an imposter. Because your pregnancy is fraught with uncertainty—hormone numbers going up and down, some spotting—and you hope with all your might that the Fertility Gods are watching and noticing how nice you're being to this pregnant woman, and they will reward you with a healthy baby. You hope they will see How Hard You Are Working.

If the Fertility Gods exist, they are Old Testament tricksters. First they give you twin heartbeats. Then you bleed and panic and go on bed rest, and at nine weeks a specialist will tell you the ultrasound has gone silent. In the logic of the body, you killed your children.

You will take one day off for the D&C, then return to work. The job and also the paperwork required for adoption. The difference is you will no longer believe. When people tell you everything happens for a reason, you will tell them to fuck off. It will be the only thing that feels right.

"The Roller Coaster" is practically an official term in adoption circles. One day you will see a picture online of a roller coaster on fire. That's a more accurate depiction of what it's like to be told by confused pregnant woman after confused pregnant woman that she wants you to raise her baby—only to have her fade away and confirm your worst fears about yourself.

Your agency promises that it's "just a matter of time" before a birthmom picks you. You can know that a needle in your arm is going to hurt but that it won't last. Still, it's always a little shocking that it hurts, and also that it doesn't last.

His name is Dash. As in the long pause before the next part. As in fast (you will meet his birthmom in December; he will be born in January). As in those dashed dreams reclaimed. As in the Olympic-level speedwalking he will begin doing at sixteen months, striking fear into your heart as he disappears behind a rack of pajamas at Target.

There is the daily work: diapering and consoling and teaching and learning. *I guess the lines on the floor do look like train tracks, don't they Dashaboo?* The day job that will pull at you like another hungry child, the creative work that pulls like a ghost. There is the work of acceptance. Your furniture is sticky. Your stomach looks like you gave birth. You pay bills late. You are always a little scared.

In addition to kidnapping and childhood cancer, you fear you will never be A Writer, because your brain is always so tired that at the end of the day, all you can do is look at Facebook and envy the achievements of your friends.

You've been here before. You've fallen for the lies of fixed identity and hard work, despite all evidence to the contrary. Sometimes you will remind yourself that there are parts you can't imagine yet. Maybe he'll be a nightmare teenager, or maybe he won't. Maybe his heart will get broken by some girl or some boy, or maybe it will sing a small lonely song to itself.

You will learn to be grateful that no one can show you the future. So forget I told you all of this, except for the part where it's going to be okay.

Sarah Anderson Wood

Lack

The making of you went
horribly wrong
but I am still at it,
some lingering construction
that defies my better sense.
Fruitless imagining.
Inside me where I cannot see
there is the site of where you were.
Cells must remain, surely,
maybe in a bloodstream
in a pocket
of organs,
hidden before I had to
let you be taken from me.

You are a lack,
an amputation,
not for the holding or viewing.
I open and fold flat
the clothes bought for you
repeated tactile memorial—
embroidered birds on pale fabric.
Each item bought with intention
of zipping you in, buttoning you up,
nursing you in.

Of your body, there will speak
two handprints, two footprints only
smaller than a doll's
pressed after they took you from me
from the tiny body I never laid eyes on.

I cannot pursue you
though I doubtless will
(touching fabric, writing words)
seeking the time of us,
the part of me where you once prodded
insistent in our revelry.

Jamie Wendt

Trying to Nurse

I
am just
a body
now.
The lactation consultant
walks in. Rebecca.
I'm topless.
I look 20 weeks pregnant
but really I'm blue as a stillbirth,
they call it "baby blues" in the new mother manual.
I am hardly post-
partum.
A black vertical line
is my stomach.
Rebecca doesn't notice
my body. Doesn't look, even.
She knows
all I am is body.
There is nothing
to see.
I need three pillows,
two sweaty hands,
a nipple shield,
a washcloth,
a timer.
And formula
in a tiny bottle
with perfectly shaped nipple
for when I fail.
I am supposed to learn
my body all over again.
Like when I was fifteen
first masturbating.
When I was seventeen
and guided a penis into me.
Like when I was twenty-six

and felt a baby kick under my skin.
And when I was twenty-seven
and my husband held up my leg
while I pushed out this child.
But all the times I learned myself
were not like this.
And now
I walk through my kitchen,
breasts leaking
bleeding and sore and the milk
isn't coming.
I have been a mother
for four days.
Already I am failing.

Robin Silbergleid

From 'Mother Time': Let Down

All these dark days and white nights, every two hours, the milk lets down. She feels the rhythm in her breasts: suck, suck, swallow. Sometimes it comes too fast, pools the side of his mouth, collects in the fat folds of his chin. Sometimes he falls asleep there, with the nipple in his mouth.

+

A diaper change. An attempt at a nap. At the hospital they said to record it all. Left breast, right breast, urine output, stool. 5 ml pumped milk offered via silver spoon. He's so small, fetal with wrinkled skin, he can't stay awake; she rubs an ice cube against his foot. He wakes cold, angry: sucks.

+

When babies are this small it is possible to weigh them before and after a feed and know precisely how much milk they have taken in. They weigh him at the hospital daily and then twenty-four hours later, then forty-eight, then wait a whole week. When she brings him home, he is four pounds eight ounces, his wrist the size of her thumb. He looks like a doll in his car seat; even the preemie clothes don't fit.

+

In the news, she reads that a baby died of dehydration because the mother didn't know she wasn't supplying enough milk; she said she fed her child around the clock and he screamed when taken from the breast.

+

In this never-ending now, the mother puts the baby to her breast. He sucks, swallows. The present is a mouthful of milk. In his belly, proteins break down to digest. Nutrients travel his blood stream: calcium, DHA, Vitamin D. Their bodies share time and space, linked by mother's milk the way they were once linked by the placenta. Infants who are breastfed adjust their body temperature and heart rate according to their mothers'. Their body clocks sync: mother time. Her body thins while he grows.

+

Another check mark on the log: wet diaper, dirty diaper, feed.

+

If the baby sleeps: dishes. If the baby sleeps: diapers. If the baby sleeps: email. If the baby sleeps: blog post. If the baby sleeps: bathtub. If the baby sleeps: laundry. If the baby refuses: rock him. If the baby refuses: swaddle him, swing him, snuggle him. If the baby refuses: try the crib, the car seat, the bed with you beside him. Give him a new diaper. Give him your left breast. Give him your right. Count the hours. Count the hours. Count the hours.

+

If there are 60 minutes in an hour and 168 hours in a week, 52 weeks in a year, how many minutes of infancy, of toddlerhood? How many spent in the rocking chair, or pacing with a baby strapped to the chest, how many in the pediatrician's waiting room, washing the spare parts of a breast pump, the innards of baby bottles? How many on the basic tasks of feeding, diapering, bathing? How many getting to and from, pushing a stroller up a hill? She's walked when she needed to drink, walked when she needed to pee. Her legs and arms are spindly. Somehow, minutes pass; somehow, she has become mother. Her breasts swell and spurt; she feels the milk let down as the baby wakes, hungry.

Shanna Powlus Wheeler

Milk Chant
For Finn

A continent and an ocean away from you,
I still made milk meant for you.

Faithful to our shared biology,
I expressed it on your schedule.

The cold throats of airport bathroom sinks
swallowed the warm ounces meant for you.

The rich soil of Maui received my richness.
I traced the island, marked my route

with white puddles soaking into red dirt.
Lava rocks bathed in milk meant for you.

I left a broken trail like the bluish stones
that mark the old King's Highway.

I poured lush upon lush, milk sweet as coconuts,
each tidal surge of letdown meant for you—

each small eruption for you but not for you—
the pump hissing your name

Heather Lewis

C.L.S. Ferguson

Weight Wait

For the first time in my life my mother weighs 17 pounds less than I do
She is down to my birth weight
Not what I weighed at my birth
What she weighed at my birth

For the first time in my life my tummy won't flatten completely
Not even if I suck in with all my might
Skip a full day of eating
Take diet pills for 10 days straight

For the first time in my life I am paying for eating whatever I want
Even months of smoothies, veggies, and lean meat
Makes not a pound of difference
I'm paying now

For the first time in my life I can't wear a size 0 in any brand
I'm considering taking up smoking again
Maybe drinking again
Too bad ephedra is illegal

Sara Epstein

Dust

she makes plans, cancels them
twists her ankle, is too alone
works and drives and forgets
why she is who she is
but she is a therapist
so must be alive
for her patients
and she is a mother
and must be alive
for her children
and she is a daughter
and must be alive
for her mother
but for her husband
she is better off dead
so she slowly dies
her apartment smells
old and musty
even after she vacuums.

Lois Marie Harrod

My Mother's Heart in Troubling Times

Her heart of brass, her heart of tin,
skin-thin heart of gold, heart of sin,

heart of glass, of flesh and flask,
her chicken-liver wussy-dither heart of hearts,

she eats it out, starts at the base, her yellow heart,
her purple heart, her crossed-and-hope-to-lie heart,

hard heart, soft and heavy heart,
light and lively heart, she eats it

bare and aching, broken, beating,
her stopped heart berating her heart-stood-still,

her standing-stone of a heart,
heart pinned to her sleeve,

heart pining for sleep,
her faint-hearted, hope-to-fly heart,

her never-catch-a-man heart,
heart in her mouth, heart in her boot,

oh her sinking heart,
skipping-a-beat heart,

the heart of those heart-to-heart-talks heart,
its cockles, its chambers, its snail

of a heart creeping along now, the heart
she never had, the heart she never had

in it, she eats it, she eats her heart out—
lets her heart do her heart some good.

Hannah Baker Saltmarsh

Ars Poetica with Rosemary

There was a time when everything was tossed
of hers or given to any family member: the shelf dust of
Shakespeare, blue dust of the Madonna, the plaster dust of
Cherokee faces as the mixed stardust someone called my
grandmother. Gold is the plains, the food we eat, the heart sometimes,
the brazenness of the gun in the new-to-them
world, but gold is the baby-wearing back, with the baby sleeping.
       My grandmother's got footage from the Holy Lands and
not the stolen land except in the resonance of her
prayer-chants. I remember she slept naked, brushed her hair
naked in the morning. Her other name was Lover.
Of her strange embattled piety, her healings under different
names with different substances, her family
knows the only time she rose to anger was in the gong of a few
clashing dishes in the sink, in the muttering of how not-mad
she was, and, if overtaken by sorrow, she made the smallest rolls,
her children could eat ten of them, each. A child she
lost like her mother buried a child is why she left her son's
last highlighted page open like a secret between them.
Nearly a century old, my grandmother, after surgery,
seated in her matrilineal silence before the raid of
thinking her thoughts, folded into herself, her spine a singular
wave of corn titled down, she just lifted the hem
of her shirt so carefully, scanning the shirt like a text,
the smooth flowery fabric she mumbled Shakespeare into,
There's rosemary, that's for remembrance. Please remember, love.
Deep memory back after the knife, the stitch like a buried accent
slips out only when drinking, or very tired. Myths like the wide picture
books in the fabric of womanly adornment, storied blankets, coats
of lost mothers you could always remember direct from the lap,
wearing a part of the story on your frame: my grandmother
reading her shirt, what is she, reading, trying to remember?

Veronica Kornberg

Fragment

I peer beneath your bed for teeth and find slippers stinking of old piss.

Half-eaten cookie, wadded tissues, melted tube of Coral Sunset.

There—that fragment of your smile, crescent of tombstones on a pink hill.

That's not possible, you say. How to help you

make sense of a world where things appear and disappear so

randomly. Guess the tooth fairy didn't want them.

Your eyes gleam. Wind wakes leaves and litter in a gray tunnel.

Your cousin's red hair: flame in the cornfield.

Hydrangeas blushing hyacinth in a lost summer. Long ago,

your whole house burned to the ground.

I fold stained slippers into the trash, rush out to buy two new pairs.

But your right foot is swollen as a sausage, drags

when you walk and knocks the slipper off. My flight is due.

You lean on the doorframe, smiling: See you tomorrow. In two months, Ma,

two months. I'll mail more slippers. I imagine shoeboxes

arriving from the blue, the way you'll cock your head

as the aid lifts them for you to see. Ancient chickadee.

Wave. It was lovely to see you, as though we're old friends, met for lunch.

　　　　I become another thing that has appeared, disappeared.

Carol Seitchik

Kitchen Talk With Mom

After dinner, we slice fig bars,
savor the sweetness. Our mouths fill
with barely the space for words—

We are on the same page, she says.
Mainly we are not.

We consume an endless amount of taste
and desire, salt then sugar, sugar then salt,
fill in with mindless talk.

In her ninety third year, the ephemera

of the body is her conversational playground—
who and what has been garnished, diminished.

She admonishes me for my lack of vanity
and my slippage from the *fashionistas*.

We slice through the last of the fleshy
fig pulp, the two of us, in our separateness—

like our beloved fig, its flower inverted into itself.
Inside, the seeds are the real fruit.

Elizabeth Ehrlich

Triple Time

Blue eggs crackle, skyroost
on a quick green branch.

Below, a rusty-feathered
robin pulling worms,

and you say *heaven*
at the window, May again

all fresh, and you say
oh, what riches,
lilac bundle in your breath.

You taught me nectar sips,
my mother bird, recall?

Once you were small
as I was then. I wrap you

in a lap robe soft as grass
and roll your chair through
singing leaves, a sarabande.

Kristin Prevallet

All The Lord's Women

My mother, Annie, had always been a misfit. In the 1950s she was a tomboy growing up in St. Louis with conservative Catholic parents who were hyper-conscious of their social standing. Forced to attend debutant balls and high social teas, she didn't come of age in a time when non-conformist women were free to live as they chose. Internalizing her anger of social mores, she spent her teenage and college years getting kicked out of Catholic all-girls reform schools (once, she slipped a lit firecracker under the Mother Superior's door). When she was old enough to see that acting out wasn't going to get her anywhere, she decided to settle down and do what her family wanted her to do—get a teaching degree, marry a nice Catholic boy, and have a child. Not a good idea. I was two years old when my father divorced her on the grounds of mental abuse and insanity (against him). Apparently she was hell to live with. Ultimately she hadn't wanted a husband and until I was finally old enough to play softball, hadn't wanted a little girl.

For the first seven years of my life Annie lived for gin and parties; I was raised by an array of babysitters and occasional visits from my father. But in 1972 Ms. magazine started appearing in the mailbox and things began to change. In these early years, Ms. ran editorials urging women to perceive their roles as caretakers and housewives as manual labor; they encouraged women to speak up against the limitations set by domineering husbands and patriarchal power structures. It's possible that the slow creeping of these ideas into the private lives of suburban families wrecked havoc on their nuclear bonds. But my mother had been battling the status quo all her life and Ms. magazine was cannon fodder. As she merged her internal conflicts with larger political struggles, she became a completely different person.

After 26 years of living a fettered existence Annie—with the grace of a weed whacker—began to shed the shackles of conformity and live a life of her choosing. In 1977 she bought a CB radio and a bright yellow and black striped Cherokee Chief Jeep which she decorated with bumper stickers: "A woman's place is in the House...and in the Senate" and "Adam was a rough draft." There was always music because she wrote her own songs (thank you Helen Reddy) and sang them loudly on the front porch while playing the six chords she knew on the guitar.

We lived in a little brick house on Canosa Court in Southwest Denver. If the idea of a home symbolized a woman's ball and chain, Annie set to work emancipating every square inch of it. She remodeled, re-rigged, and re-wired every socket, fixture, and floorboard in the house. She replaced all the plumbing, pruned the trees, axed the stumps, and built a fireplace (which of course involved her cutting a hole in the roof). When something was broken she didn't just fix it—she rigged it, soldered it, or duck-taped it. Experts were called and the instructions read only when all else failed. There was no tool built by any man that she couldn't figure out how to use. Chain saws, circle saws, sanders, drills, and ratchets—these were the contents of my mother's armoire.

She was a trail blazer, but she wasn't alone. She became a co-member of the Sisters of Loretto and found in these women a religious community with a passionate and relentless commitment to social justice. Summertime weekends in Annie's backyard were all about barbecue, beer, and nuns sitting around talking politics. Once the sun went down, this spirited group of women would eat homemade pie with three different choices of ice cream. My mother would play songs on her guitar and everyone would sing along. At 10 p.m. on the dot, everyone left. As my mother liked to say, "nuns like to drink beer but they also like to get up really early to pray."

And there was lots to pray about in the 1980s, the decade of excess: death squads were slaughtering villages in Central America and several of the Sisters of Loretto were traveling to San Salvador to bear witness; The Iran-Contra scandal unfolded a cloak of cover-ups and the U.S. bombed Libya in retaliation for terrorist plots.

But I didn't care about any of that.

I didn't care about the failed rescue attempt of American hostages in Iran or that unemployment was at the highest rate since 1940. I didn't notice that IBM introduced the personal computer or that the chemical disaster in Bhopal killed 13,000 people. Rather, I cried when Vanessa Williams won the Miss America Pageant and thought it was incredibly unfair that I was forbidden to watch *Baywatch*.

I was dedicated to boycotting grapes to support the farm workers, but I resented having to constantly defend my love of *Seventeen* magazine and Princess Diana. My desires for what I considered to be a normal life were constantly being questioned. I wonder now why my mother didn't see that our childhoods had a lot in common—we were both expected to conform to a lifestyle that was of someone else's design.

As a teenager, my rebellion against my mother was total. But unlike the rebellious kids of my generation who were listening to punk and ripping their tee-shirts, I was reading *The Preppy Handbook* and trying out for the Glee Club (never made it). I wanted to be an upper class popular girl but had no idea how to do it because my cultural references were completely off-kilter and I had been raised to be what Annie was denied to be by her parents: a tomboy. Talk about gender trouble.

My mother and I tried really hard to meet in the middle. I had a crush on Superman and she wanted to be him, so we both liked Christopher Reeves. I refused to scoot under a car to replace the boot on the axle shaft, but I didn't mind tanning on my lawn chair while handing her tools to fix the lawn mower. I refused to hook a worm and I know she was disappointed that I had no passion for fishing; but she didn't stop me from sitting quietly on the river's edge reading Victoria Holt romances while she caught a cooler full of trout.

I remember with certitude that I desperately wanted to get out of her crazy world and create my own. But I couldn't have imagined how catastrophically this transition would unfold. Just as she had secured her footing in this self-created and empowered reality, she was diagnosed with a vicious breast cancer. She was convinced that it happened during a volley ball game at the local community center in which she was the only woman—and a man from the opposing team slammed the ball with all his strength right into her left breast.

She fought that cancer for five years. She had two mastectomies, but refused to wear prostheses. Instead, she told people that she was glad her breasts were gone because they got in the way when she tried to run bases in softball. She didn't care about the snickers from gas station attendants, or the men she embarrassed. "May I help you sir?" they would ask after glancing at a stout, short-haired person in lumberjack attire. "No thank you, ma'am," she would sweetly reply. Once, to my horror, she mowed the lawn shirtless, her double scars exposed for the neighbors to see. But Annie wasn't bothered. If people stared at her, she would smile and wave.

She died in 1986 at the age of 46, and the nuns and I scattered her ashes across three mountains in Colorado. But at the Loretto convent in Nerinx, KY, there is a graveyard that sits on top of a cow pasture with the stations of the cross lined up to mark the entrance. Her tombstone is at this place and it reads: "Sister Annie Prevallet. Choose Life." This gravestone and its epitaph give me the enormous satisfaction of being able to tell people that my mother was a nun. But it wasn't until now as I surpass the age my mother was when she died that I began to think about what the epitaph from Deuteronomy 30:19 meant to her:

I call heaven and earth to record this day against you, that I have set before you life and death, blessing and cursing: therefore choose life, that both thou and thy seed may live.

The official reading says that this is a passage about choosing the right path to serve God and obey the church. But Annie took it to mean the opposite of servitude. I now realize that although my childhood was weathered by Annie's struggle for autonomy and identity, I received a powerful gift from her that this passage conveys: the deep knowing that even when the world and all its forces are against you, the seed that chooses life is the one that is growing. The live or die choice is choosing to follow the part of you that blossoms—no matter how chaotically—into the rest of your life.

Matt Hohner

Cord

I am eight years old, running from the living
room to the dining room, under the taut
phone cord and into the kitchen. My mother
is talking with a girlfriend from Sweet
Adelines. She's chain smoking in the slat
wooden swivel chair at the end of the grey
formica counter. The warm June afternoon
light spilling from the back yard into the hazy
row house beckons, but I stay inside to be near
her. She talks for hours on the phone, her lifeline,
drawing lit end after lit end into her lungs. The
coiled line stretches and tightens with her tone
as it follows her into another room when she
needs to whisper. I duck under that cord a half
dozen times for the attention she won't give me
before she sends me out into the yard with the dog.
How much longer would I hear her voice in that
kitchen, yank desperately on the line that keeps
us apart, that keeps her tethered to our home?
How much longer would the smoke of her
conversations linger in the air, a sure sign
of something burning in that house?

Gail Newman

Heritage

A mother, braiding, says, *Be still.*
Says, *Here is bread. Eat.*
You are tired. Rest. Take this umbrella.
Outside it is raining.

The mother closes, at night, the door.
She rolls down her stockings,
unsnaps the brassiere.
Turns down her side of the bed.
The father, already asleep, does not wake.
Some nights he may moan. Others, shout
out. Then he walks the long hall.
If it is summer, he goes into the yard
where the moon is full, spilling
as if from a bucket of warm milk
its luminous light.

Indoors the child sleeps,
dreaming of the blue mist above the ocean
and the blue velvet dress her father
stitched on a treadled Singer,
dipping his foot down on the pedal,
guiding the fabric between his hands,
the needle zipping in and out like a bee
inside the honey of a flower.

Laura Page

Freda and Songda

My grandmother used to tell my dad
to beat approaching storms if they were out.
He'd grin, remembering. *Beat it, kid,* she'd say, *I'll be along.*
Freda was no exception. '62's buxom typhoon had taken off
from the green glass ballroom of the Pacific, hiked her skirts,
was running to Gold Beach. *Run home.*
He tried to run. Instead he rode, skidding
and lifting on her dirty hems.

As a teen, I courted Freda's children, the
gale force winds annually skirting Klamath Falls,
snapping their sashes against broken sidewalks,
all seduction.

I wanted to lead.
I took the lid off a trash can once, and brandished it,
gangly matador, at their bird-breaking skirts. The gales
were sharp-toed, but all they did was kick my
steel, laugh in the ally.

This evening, the National Weather Service warns
typhoon Songda is having a courtesan's conniption, like her
grandmother Freda's in '62.
The green glass ballroom slammed back, she's
running hard for Ashland. *Beat it,* I hear myself saying
as my son hangs back. I know he'd tempt her to a dance.

Meredith Trede

Riding Away

My mother rode
up and over
hurdles. Away
from her father's
fists and flailing
temper. Her riding crop
clutched, unused,
as her body urged
the animal on
city scenes and sounds
fell far behind.

She rode and fell,
rode and fell, 'til
finally pregnant,
with me, she neither
rode again, nor,
to keep me safe,
let me ride.
I fled for a life
away from her fear.

So far past
her death, in dream
I finger the nap
of her long-lost
soft suede riding
coat, straining
to inhale
its musky scent
as I slip into
the silken lining,
snug the belt tight.

Tom Holmes

Imagined Scenario 6: Birth Mother's Careers

You entered Manhattan
as a Moth Ball Inc. marketer.
You designed campaigns

for widows in big houses,
you promoted lavender,
lemon, and linen scented balls.

You were dubbed Moth Woman
by *Scientific American*
and *Fortune*, and the CEO

position was offered to you,
along with controlling stocks
and salary enough

to stuff a mattress each month.
You slept comfortably as hungry
children ate your balls

and fell into encephalopathic
depression, as mothball-filled houses
burned down. You rose

to the occasion and entered
a marble-playing tournament
with your mothballs and won.

That was before the lawyers, OSHA,
and criminal and civil lawsuits.
You ate a handful of balls

to prove your case. You won
but were asked to demit. You left
behind a trail of your rotted teeth.

You couldn't eat popcorn, caramel apples,
peanut brittle, or ice. You hungered.
As your mattress cash-flow finances depleted,

you invented a new campaign
as the pink-skirted tooth fairy
specific to my adopted home.

You slid down the chimney,
removed my teeth, and left
me a quarter when you could
have left a resignation note.

Nina Bannett

Making Art

Hang me on the wall the way you did when I was a little girl,
lines of thin pencil on paper echoing my skin behind the chair.
I was sleeping, my pose a rag of outline and hair. Later your art became abstract.
People became trees and leaves. I helped you gather them each fall. We looked
on the ground for important patterns. Talked about the formation of snowflakes.
No two look alike. *Fractals prove the presence of God*, you told me in so many words.
Your art meant you wanted to be re-made. Your studio locked. I watched you
install the eyelet and hook. I could see through a crack. The wall was seven feet high.
You left the house for classes. Proclaimed yourself an artist with a different name.
First and last. A Christian name that exposed your real desires. No one asked
why you chose this name and not another. Why you chose to move away from people.
Turn towards leaves and trees. Re-planting yourself as an artist with different desires.
Hanging your hopes on exhibitions. On paper threads and watercolors.
Making yourself an artist without a human subject.
Re-making yourself without me as art.

Tsaurah Litzky

My Mother's Work

It was my mother's work that taught me and is still teaching me how to keep myself together. I do not mean her housework, the fine meals or the immaculate floors. It is the work of her spirit, steadfast and strong, that is my example.

My mother's name was Ruth. Like the biblical Ruth she was stoic in the face of obstructions, she just kept going. She never gave in to hysteria or weeping or "Woe is me's." She was tough and did not believe in self-pity. She considered it her job as a mother to teach me to be responsible for myself. She was very fond of homilies, among her favorites were *actions speak louder than words*, and *look before you leap*.

When I was five and on my first roller skates, I fell, scraping my knee on the crack in the sidewalk in front of the Finkel's house. It was bleeding. I was weeping like it was the end of the world as I skated back to our stoop. My mother was sitting there talking with our neighbor, Mimi. My mother stopped mid-sentence, scooped me up in her arms, carried me into our house, into the bathroom. She sat me on the toilet seat.

Then she took off my skates and drying my tears with toilet paper, she said, "Stop your bawling! Never feel sorry for yourself, it could have been worse. Learn to look before you leap or you will never know what's ahead of you." She hugged and kissed me, then damped a gauze pad and showed me how to gently clean the dirt and blood from the cut. She let me finish cleaning the cut and showed me how to paint the cut with Mercurochrome and make a bandage out of gauze pads and Band-Aids. "So you'll know what to do if you fall down and cut yourself again," she told me. "Now come into the kitchen and help me make dinner. Tomorrow you can go skating again."

I wish I could say I never or even hardly ever felt sorry for myself. I tend to bend in the other direction, towards self-flagellation. Though now, seventy years later, I remember how to clean and dress a cut like an ace, and I can mostly catch myself before bursting into tears in public and making a sorry display of myself.

My mother did not believe in crying in public. She told me so when I was twelve and starting to develop. "Do not cry in front of people. They will think you are weak and crazy, a hysteric like your cousin Marcia. Try to do your crying in private except at funerals, then crying is okay." Indeed, the only time I ever saw my mother cry was at the funeral of her favorite brother, Julie. He had a sudden heart attack while playing tennis. He was sixty-two and she was sixty. My mother weeping, rushed into my father's arms.

"We've all gotten so old, Jerry, we've gotten so old," she cried. He pulled his handkerchief from his pocket to dry her tears. She grabbed it from his hand, wiped her face and went to comfort my Uncle Julie's wife, Clara, who was crying uncontrollably.

My mother, the stoic, also knew how to celebrate. When I was thirteen she gave me a pink plastic Schick electric razor to shave the new hair growing under my arms and the hair growing on my legs. It was shaped like a shell and slightly larger than the palm of my hand. She got one for herself too. She said, " All those years of using your father's razor and messy shaving cream, now we are both modern women."

Later the same day, leaving my five-year old brother to play with Harvey next door, my mother took me to downtown Brooklyn to May's department store, now gone, to buy me my first brassiere. We took different size bras into the Try-On room and determined I was a perfect size thirty-two double AA. My mother, encouraging me to develop my own taste, let me pick out three bras. I chose one pink, one flesh tone and one white trimmed with lace. Then we went to the Chock-Full-of-Nuts next to the May's to celebrate my approaching womanhood. We had cream-cheese sandwiches on raisin nut bread. I felt so grown up sitting next to her at the counter and talking about grown-up things like me going away to college one day. "You can be anything you want," my mother told me. "You are smart enough and I'm proud of you."

"Celebrating special occasions like your first bra are important," she said. "It means you will be a woman soon." I had not yet gotten my period like a lot of the other girls in my class. I felt left out when they talked about periods in the locker rooms after gym class. My mother assured me, "You will get it in a few months." She was right.

I never doubted my mother; I had never caught her in a lie. "Celebrations remind you why you should be happy," she said. She enjoyed throwing parties for birthdays, anniversaries, graduations. She cooked, cleaned, baked and sometimes decorated the living room with crepe paper streamers. As I grew older she involved me more with the preparations. Working with her, preparing for our parties, she taught me *one thing at a time* and *everything has its place.* I have tried using these maxims to manage my wild emotional and romantic lives. As with the other life skills she taught me, I have had limited success, but that limited success has offered me enough real protection to enable me to move forward into my life.

I did not cry at my mother's funeral. I gave the eulogy and afterwards hosted in my parents' apartment a *shiva kiddish* I made for my mother containing her favorite dishes. So many people kept coming to pay their respects.

Much later, after the last guest had gone, my father was sleeping, snoring loudly, in their bedroom. I sat in the kitchen in the chair that had been my mother's, amid the debris of the party. I started to cry and cry. I couldn't stop myself. I missed my mother. I wanted to touch her. Her body was in a pine box under the earth, but where was she, her spirit? It is not part of the Jewish religion to believe in heaven with angels or hell with fires. My mother agreed, "No one ever came back to tell me about it," she always said.

After a while I stopped crying. The kitchen was a mess. One thing at a time. I bagged the garbage from the garbage pails and put it in the hall for the super. I rinsed the serving dishes that were in the sink and put them in the dishwasher. I washed my hands and face with the Ivory soap that was always in a crystal dish besides the sink. Then I went into my mother's sewing room and lay down on the studio couch that was next to her boxes of material and threads.

Margaret Rozga

Mama Keeps Spring Under Control

It grows wild.

Clean, oil the shears,
get out the ladder,
square the hedge.

Draw blade smoothly
just below the tangle
of new growth. Rake.

Discard the fallen.

Cheryl Boyce-Taylor

When Her Child Dies
For Malik

A mother does not know her heart
will leap out of her chest

with such intense force
it will cause a rebellion

she does not know
that her hands will be numb for two weeks

she does not know
her sugar will jump to over five hundred

even though she has not eaten in two days
she will come to distrust her universe

her black eyed susans' her sweet williams'
the soil she loves to squish her toes in

sun hugging her aching shoulders
moon scurrying across her worn window sill

she will mistrust them all

when her child dies
friends will come every day with milk, honey

cheese, red wine, modelo, spelt bread, & ginger jam
she will not remember their touch

only their eyes glossed over with tears
she does not know

she will stop speaking to his father
and threaten to sue him

her hair will fall out in clumps
she will lose big spaces of memory

when her child dies

a woman will fight for her sanity
she will travel to Anguilla beg Yemaya to bring him back

her friends Jessie and Eric
will meet her there

she will love them
in a new way after that

they will keep an eye on her
as the ocean swells she listen for his laughter

she will press her face in the damp earth
she will call his name again and again

Malik, Malik,
Malik.

Mary Di Lucia

Everything is going to be all right

Guido van der Werve, "Everything is going to be alright" 2007
16 mm film transferred to video. Object number 70.2009
Museum of Modern Art, New York

'Everything is going to be alright'

That's what the little plaque at the Museum of Modern Art says: *Everything is going to be alright.* The man is running in front of a ship, an icebreaker, wearing only his frail coat, his slippery-bottomed shoes. Is the icebreaker chasing him? Is he decoying it? Why doesn't he get out of the way. It tails him mercilessly. He is only a few skittering steps in front of it. A run-walk. And yet there is something soothing about the almost running, the impending icebreaker potentially plowing over him and plowing him under. He stops, almost but doesn't quite look back, half-runs again. Walks quickly a little to one side, to the other. The wind whips his hair. He wipes his forehead. Half glances over a shoulder. Walks fast. Almost runs.

You notice, over time, that the ship is always the same distance away from the man. It never catches up. He keeps skittering ahead, just enough, just barely enough. He never makes ground but never loses any. Does the ship even know he is there? Its radar is trawling the atmosphere. Is anyone inside the ship? Does a human eye look out and see him?

Your son loves this exhibit. He dances in the shadow he makes against the wall, as if he were part of the dance between the man and the icebreaker. In and out of the light cast by the invisible projector.

Where is the man going? he asks.

Home, he answers himself.

The man is going home. When you do go home, it is the icebreaker he talks about. He wants to go back to what he calls *'the Modern Museum.'* He wants to see the icebreaker. Did the icebreaker get the man yet? Did the man make it home?

You particularly like that the icebreaker video is called *Everything is going to be alright*: it is either optimism, or it is a lie. Either way, it comforts you, the title.

The second time, and the third, the third time you go all the way to the MoMA on a Friday night with an almost three year old, a task which is your work as a mother, you begin to register, slowly, what the real problem is here. The way it has been staged, the icebreaker and the man are head-to-head with the viewer. Not only is the man perpetually pursued by the icebreaker, he is also perpetually trapped between the icebreaker and you, as you stand there in front of the image and watch. The distances between the man, the icebreaker, and you, the viewer, do not vary. Thus it is you, as you watch, that the icebreaker is approaching. You and your boy, and all the people in the museum, the people in the stairwell, and on the stairs, those who stop and those who keep walking by, all menaced by the icebreaker. The same margin of safety, the frame of slight ice, the watery border of video footage, which also seems to be vanishing but never vanishes, is all that protects both the man and you. And it is coming closer. You have been watching and not getting out of the way. Everything is going to be all right. *Alright*, it says. Misspelled.

You feel sorry for the icebreaker. Its work, like yours, will never be done. It will never reach the man. It will never reach the shore, or home. It will never leave the wall, the frame; it will not get a chance to fulfill its destiny of obliterating you, or your little boy, or the man, or anyone. It is a tiresome task, its never-ending approach. At the end of the video loop, no one is any closer to a resolution. The little margin of safety, protecting the icebreaker, the man, you, it stays the same. What is it that lets us know how it is going to turn out? Just that title: *Everything is going to be alright*. When, how, it does not say.

Everything is going to be all right.

The man's lack of a coat and proper shoes.
Your boy. You. The inadequate provision. That which cannot be protected from. That which will plow you under.

Everything is going to be all right.

"It is a rotating collection," the guard explains, the fourth time you return to the museum, when the little video projector, the man, the icebreaker are gone. The wall is blank. The child wails. "We move things in and out."

Everything is going to be alright

It is gone.

Judith Lichtendorf

Sometimes I Have Bad Thoughts

One

I am at work.

My son, Ben, is walking home from school. He is eight, almost nine. His school is three blocks away from our apartment. I'm not a baby, mom, he says, I can go home by myself. So our housekeeper, Patsy, is waiting for him there. It's a warm day in October, a little after three in the afternoon. I see Ben so clearly, my adored one, a beautiful child, blond, blue-eyed, a little tall for his age, a little on the thin side, a little messy after his school day, leaky ball point ink on his fingers, shirt sticking out, sweater shoved into his back pack. He's thinking about something – I can see he's drifting, not dawdling exactly, just drifty, thinking, paying attention to what's inside his mind. Perhaps he's thinking about his birthday and what presents he will get; he wants a dog very badly. Perhaps he's thinking about that, could his wish possibly come true? Could he really get a puppy? He's imagining the puppy, tumbling and yipping, a Dalmatian puppy? A collie? Now he's two blocks away from our apartment house, then one block away, and now a man walks by, with a boxer on a leash, and Ben smiles at the dog and says, hello pup, just like his dad does when his dad sees a dog that he likes. Hello pup. And the owner says, you

Sometimes I Have Bad Thoughts

can pet her, and Ben pets the dog, she sniffs his hand and, Goodbye pup, Ben says, and the man and dog continue on, and Ben keeps walking, now he's really dreaming about a dog, maybe a boxer like this one and he's crossing the street and a navy blue Mercedes Benz is turning the corner and the driver is as distracted as Ben is and doesn't see him until it's too late and Ben is up in the air and then smashed to the ground and the car stops with a terrible screech of brakes and Ben is flat, his face on its side with a black worm of blood trickling out from his nose.

Two

I am in the air, circling. Soon, but not soon enough, I'll be at LaGuardia, standing in the taxi line.

It is eight o'clock at night. My son Ben is finished with dinner, he's done his homework. The housekeeper, Patsy, is rinsing dishes and loading the dishwasher. There is a key in the door, it's Joe, my husband, Ben's stepfather. Joe's been cheering up a client who just got fired. Hey, you never know where the guy is going to land, and what kind of business he might be able to deliver. Joe is smart.

Sometimes I Have Bad Thoughts

Hi Patsy, he says.

Then, hey there chief, to Ben. What's shakin', baby?

It's their ritual. Ben always says, Slap me five. Ben and Joe do palms, and Joe moves to the bar. Do you want a drink, he asks Ben, or do you have homework?

Also part of their routine. Ben giggles.

Joe makes a drink. Patsy has a sandwich waiting for him.

Patsy gets Ben bathed and brushed, presents him for a kiss. Is mom coming home tonight, Ben wants to know. Yes, Joe says, but late, you'll be asleep, you'll see her in the morning.

Patsy leaves.

The Giants are on TV.

Joe stands up to make another drink. He trips on the coffee table and falls on top of his glass which slices into his neck and he bleeds to death while Ben sleeps, and I am finally first in the taxi line and I give the driver my address and sit back and relax.

Kyle Potvin

Falling Asleep While Reading

Last night I slept with Murdoch
under my back,
Eliot nudging my hip,
Lessing licking my lip
like a cat.

They argued all night,
waking me
with their strong language.
I tried not to listen.
I needed to think things through,

figure out how to correct
my stumblings
which produced a child
who believes nothing
I do.

Morning comes slowly.
Through the fog-
filled glass of my room,
the trees remind me
of the *Himalayas of tedium.*

Regret sits on me
like a toddler.
When I was my son's age,
I read much,
understood some.

I still don't understand much,
not the building and rebuilding
of sand by water.
Nor these birches that bow low
with snow and never break.

There are the blueberries.
One day this summer
they will burst open
although it may be another year
when I pick none.

Libby Maxey

Watch this.
I did.
Not always
though.

I watched
the toy theatricals
the snapping demonstration
all the proud performances of being.

I watched you
fall backwards down the hill
and split your head.

I watched the stillness
of your reading, sleeping,
sitting in the yard
staring at the day.

It was better not to watch
at some point,
not to be an audience
for every mess
and argument.

It was better not to be
the eye of the panopticon
when you were longing
for another's gaze.

Patrice Boyer Claeys

Lament For The Unchanging

"…I can't go on, I'll go on." - Samuel Beckett

I clean your house,
pick up the flakes of fake
leather littering the floor
by your couch,
scrape the black sludge
from the tub where your son
can't play, or stretch out,
crown to toes, and float
away.

I pour the soup I've simmered
into snap-its, stuff peppers I've cut
with jack-o-lantern smiles
to match the Facebook post you loved,
turn your crop of wilting
bee-swarmed tomatoes
into pasta sauce to feed you
when the Food Stamps run out.

I've haunted sales for 12-month, 2T,
now size 8 pants and shirts, coats
and fluffy towels that end up stained
in damp piles on the closet floor.

And cats—first 2, now 4,
and then 2 dogs—I cart to low-cost clinics,
each time hoping there will be no more.

It seems I can't escape you, can't salve
your sting ray heart,
my smudged
and lovely
daughter

of the shattering.

Carole Mertz

Listening to Silences in Santa Fe

En boca cerrada no entran moscas
Old Spanish saying
(Flies don't enter a closed mouth)

Conchalina sits on my desk, her straw wisps rising out of her head. She's pretty, yet disturbing. Imparting a serious lesson, she first spoke to me in a beautiful craft shop in Santa Fe.

My son, Jay, and I experienced our early days together in a small apartment in College Point, Queens. Those days, while working one full-time and two part-time jobs, I was preoccupied with keeping us fed and clothed and overseeing Jay's schoolwork. Trips to the zoo or amusement parks were rare. I didn't bake cookies for his school birthday parties, was lucky to attend final day school ceremonies, and never took a day off from work to take him sight-seeing or on a ferry ride to Staten Island.

Conchalina enters, with her mystery—

I.

Antoinette of the mountains,
south and west,
sculpted a figurine
I cannot comprehend.

Done in brown and white
it's crafted of mud
from the clay of Santa Fe.
And there, on a visit, I bought her.

Years after our New York days, Jay and I are on vacation. We enter a shop that borders on the square in the center of Santa Fe. I notice worshippers entering the St. Francis Basilica across the way. This is the very church the priest, in Cather's historical romance, is thought to have founded.

We feel a joy and lightness, being together. Maybe that's because of the colorful craft fair taking place on the square. In small cubicles, the artisans display silver rings, hats, bracelets, tablecloths, terra cotta vases, crosses, paintings done in the deep purples of Southwestern landscapes. We meander past the exhibits, aware of the vibrant creativity surrounding us.

In the shop, the owner explains something important about the little sculpture I'd just bought. But I'm too excited to listen, excited about where I am, excited to be able to purchase something as frivolous as this figurine.

For decades Jay and I lived on opposite sides of the continent and we'd spent very little time together. Now, with his business established, he was free to arrange a holiday for us. We're easy together, though it was not always so. We share much, but are also quite comfortable with silences.

Conchalina, however, speaks her message. She speaks, but still puzzles me.

II.

Little Pueblo figurine,
teach me, through your crafted eyes
and mouth,
the need for silence
or for speech.

She sits there, brown
and clean-white, with legs crossed
and holding a mobile phone.
Looking upward, (mocking perhaps)
her mouth is open,
always open.

I see Conchalina talking on her phone. As we trek through the crowds I think, were I to lose my cellphone I'd truly be lost here. My link to this town is solely through my son. I'm pleased that I can lean on him, were I to need help. The sunshine, the bright tablecloth I'd purchased, the wide silver bracelet he'd bought, and the happy crowds around us, add to our fun.

Through the din of eager artisans, I anticipate the meal we'll share that evening in the old town. Meanwhile, we enjoy viewing things we don't need, having fun, all the same.

The sculpture concerns me—the figure, her mouth open. A friend constantly cautions me, "If your mouth is open, you can never learn anything." Have I spoken so often without thinking?

Today, I find silence allows me to be receptive to Jay, not critical as I've been in the past. It offers me the capacity to handle anything he might tell me: ways he suffers, perhaps, or satisfactions he derives from accomplishments. It's a long time since his college days when we almost lost contact with each other. In a rebellious state, he'd severed telephone connections. *Conchalina, with open mouth, don't tell me that wasn't a close call!*

III.

Antoinette, the artist, (in the shop)
had explained the injunction
against speaking. Yet here sits
Conchalina, her mouth open
wide. (Someone should admonish her!)

When to be silent, when to speak—
easy to miscalculate.
Conchalina, my little sculpted model,
had I attended more closely,
I might have gained
your mystery.

In this old Royal City, I enjoy the strong Spanish influence. The Basilica stands lofty in its not-quite-buried history. The spirit of the older indigenous culture, lying deep within the clay of the pueblo hillsides surrounding the town, also exhibits a strong, silent presence.

Jay explains the demands of his new position. I'm proud of what he's achieved. In the past, for about five years, he'd been one step short of homeless. Having lost his father at an early age, he'd had a difficult time establishing himself. But in spite of hardships, he'd pulled through and become the tall, lanky and self-possessed engineer he is today. At dinner, I give him my full attention, listening with gratitude and thinking chiefly about his persistence, the trait he'd gleaned from his grandfather.

Conchalina's a mystery. I can't quite discern her meaning. We go through life not knowing when to be silent and when to speak. Maybe that's her message, that we can't know the appropriate times. Nevertheless, I enjoy the way she connects me to this ancient pueblo culture.

Jay interrupts my reverie. "Mom, wanna take in the Georgia O'Keeffe tomorrow?" I answer in the affirmative. Thanks to the kindness of the passing years, I feel we've arrived; at last we've learned how to spend recreational time together.

Comprehending Conchalina's message may take a few more years. Meanwhile, I position her on my bureau, glancing at her now and then as I proceed to make my diary entry.

Matthew Sharpe

Opera

Todd's mother's diabetes caused her placenta to deteriorate prematurely so Todd was born retarded, but he outgrew it. By age four he was singing. By six he was an international opera star. He didn't speak till age eight, when he said, "I don't want to sing opera in public anymore, it's humiliating." He was a fast runner. One fine day two years after his last singing engagement, his mother, Sandy, drove him down to the track at the high school and timed him in the mile—tenth fastest time in the world for a boy in his age group. But she knew better than to enter him in a worldwide track and field meet, having learned her lesson when she'd cancelled his last singing tour and was slaughtered on the internet, which triggered a year-long drinking binge that led to the loss of her left leg below the knee, what with the diabetes. Plus the stress of having a peculiar child. He continued to speak almost not at all except to himself, in his bedroom, at night, saying things like, "Don't worry, I am watching over you, and before long I will come to rescue you from this unsatisfactory life." She puzzled over who in that speech was imaginary, the speaker, the listener, both, or neither, and concluded that it didn't matter, the meaning was clear. She told him she'd heard him talking in his room and asked what it was all about. He looked at her in silence, a form of contact despite his thoughts and feelings being unknown to her. And not the only form. He smiled at her when she placed before him each meal that she had prepared, and every third night or so until age twelve, he climbed into her bed and clung to her as the survivor of a wrecked cruise ship clings to a passing chunk of wood. Sandy stopped drinking and was fitted for a prosthetic leg that allowed her to go jogging with Todd—she was quite fast too, and still young, and through controlled diet and exercise had eliminated her illness. On the morning of his fourteenth birthday they were out running in a field when there appeared a dark, medium-sized dog. The dog greeted Todd warmly and vice versa. "Hi poochie, hi poochie, hi poochie," six more words than he'd spoken to her all week. Watching this communion, she failed to notice the arrival of the dark girl who owned the dog. Todd straightened up from petting him and looked at the girl. She looked back. Sandy saw that they had never met before, but, as if along wires between their two pairs of eyes, they agreed they would know each other. "Let's go for a run with him," the girl said, and Sandy's immobilized feet said that the invitation did not include her. Todd picked up a stick, and with the strength and agility that still surprised her, he threw it far down the field. The dog took off after it at top speed. Todd and the girl went after the dog. The girl and the dog, neither of whose names she knew, were also very fast. The three of them stopped long enough for Todd to wrestle the stick from the dog's mouth and throw it again. They sling-shotted out after it, and so on. Alone in the field, the mother watched her son and his new companions become smaller and smaller until she could not see them.

Wither The Leaf

They sat together by the pool under the Tuscan sky. One was a fading beauty, the other in the bloom of youth. All eyes were on the youthful one, chatty and charming, while the older woman suffered unaccountable bouts of sadness accompanied by tears.

"Cluck, cluck" her friends fussed. But there was nothing to do. It was just time wafting in the wind, turning the pages, spinning the wheel. They made jokes and told stories, but the woman hummed softly to herself, testing the Italian language. The strange low, slow sounds were a vocal affirmation, a commitment to presence. A moan.

Her daughter, who was approaching the age of twenty-three, tossed her long hair about and dove into the pool, where the stone foundations of the fifteenth century house met with the terraced descent of fresh lavender and ancient rock. She was a sleek mermaid, splaying her arms above her head and frolicking. Everything about her tingled and shivered. She was buoyant and light. She played while her mother professed a headache and climbed the long stairs to her room where she was overtaken by a bout of melancholia.

The trip from America to Italy, which had been years in the making, was twofold. The woman's daughter had recently graduated college. This was a celebratory adventure. The fact that they were staying with the woman's friend, who had been her lover forty years before when the two of them were in college, was a footnote. Each had married someone else but kept a commitment to remain friends.

While everyone flirted and chatted in the company of weekend guests she wondered where all the time had gone and how little of it she had left. She reflected on her youth, her passions and then how she had become a mother. She recalled the labor of childhood when each was the center of the other's world. She thought how all her children were grown now, and stared vacantly into the horizon. These thoughts caused her to languish while everyone else drank Campari, toasting the future. She could not help but compare her age to the younger ones among them. She felt spent and exhausted, like every experience had already happened and there was no reason to bother with anything new. The sun did not agree with her and neither did the food. She was pale and bloated, rubbing her swollen ankles by the side of her bed while the others soaked up the afternoon sun. She could hear them laughing and she was jealous.

Falling into a long sleep, she awoke and observed the fading afternoon light turning shades of pink across the distant mountains. She could hear movement in the rest of the house on the floors below and began to dress for another arduous dinner where she would drink more than her share of prosecco before passing out into another dull sleep.

That night they drove to Cortona. After collecting cashmere and leather, they ordered *appertivos* and toasted their spoils. This was how their time together unfolded, day after day until a week had passed. Then, on one of their trips, the woman caught sight of a tiny shop on the main square in the hilltop village. The store was etched into a cave and was owned by a man whose father and grandfather were also jewelers. In the window, a beautiful handmade necklace of heavy silver with a gold coin gleamed against a dark velvet display. While the others in her group argued over the quality of leather in the dark bowels of a biker shop, she slipped away to try on the necklace. The kindly clerk fussed over the woman, describing the style of craftsmanship, its age, and the story of the coin of Cortona. This was the way she usually fawned over her daughter and the lavished attention felt good.

She stood looking at herself in the mirror and thanked the clerk. Then, she plunked down one hundred and ninety euros for the chain and seventy-seven for the coin. After, the woman stood on the corner holding the coin in her hand. She felt elegant and proud. Her daughter, who was usually loving and attentive, was cross on this night and did not approach her as the others waved towards the restaurant where they had planned to meet.

Another dinner of too much wine and heavy meats meant she did not sleep well. This was often the case. She awoke at four a.m. A mixture of emotions lay just below the surface when the time came to say goodbye. They said farewell to her friend's wife. Goodbye to the large, vertical empty green mountain just beyond the villa's border. Goodbye to the wild wet fountain, the trees, and the bay leaves. Then she said goodbye to her friend of forty years, kissing him lightly on the lips. In that moment, they lingered long enough for all the sweetness to come flooding back, transporting her to the place where time stands still—eternally. Taking her daughter's hand, she bade her hurry so they would not miss their train.

Heather Haldeman

That Girl

At a family dinner a few months ago, our son-in-law, Doug, announced that he'd bought tickets to the Arroyo Seco Weekend Music Festival for my husband, Hank, for Father's Day.

"I got tickets for the whole family, too," Doug added, knowing that he and Hank along with our other children share a love of blues and classic rock. "I thought it'd be a fun thing for all of us."

Hank was thrilled. "This is great!"

Me, I'm more into Broadway tunes and movie soundtracks. I like quiet dinners. Going to restaurants. Movies at the iPic. I'm not a concertgoer. Never have been. Just never been that girl.

"Wow, so nice of you, Doug," I said, reaching for the pepper mill, already trying to figure a way out.

My daughter, Hilary, eyed me. "Mom, Tom Petty's headlining. I know you like him."

"Oh, I do," I nodded. She was right. I like Tom Petty, but, a music festival? Not my thing.

And I had known about this Arroyo Seco Music Festival to be held down at The Rose Bowl just blocks from our home. I'd spoken out against it months ago at a meet-and-greet with our Pasadena Mayor. "I know it brings in revenue for the city," I'd argued, "but our neighborhood will be overrun with traffic for two whole days."

"You sure you wanna go?" Hank asked later while we cleaned up the dinner dishes.

How could I not when everyone else in my family was going… "I'm in," I replied.

"Really?" he asked.

I tried to sound convincing. "Oh, yeah. Definitely."

As the weekend grew near, I began to dread the thought of little blue port-a-potties, sitting on the ground, and crowds gathered in the heat.

To add to it, our daughter, Hilary, requested that I make it festive before we all go. "We'll park at our house and walk down," she said. "Maybe Mimosas? Some fun food?"

Mimosas at 1:30? I can't possibly. It's daytime! "Sure! Sounds fun," I lied.

My friend, Wendy, told me to loosen up. "Have a Mimosa," she said. "Relax and have some fun." It's something she seems to say to me a lot.

"Just be happy to be with your children," my friend, Margaret, told me the day before the festival. "You're so lucky they all live here – and that they want you to be with them!"

My friends were right. Loosen up, I told myself.

Instead of enjoying the moment and heeding their advice the next day, I nursed a low-fat yogurt while cutting up more watermelon and pouring chips into a bowl, scolding myself for not putting the orange juice in a proper pitcher. While at the kitchen island Hank and the rest of my family were having a ball, partaking of the spread. Pouring. Sipping. Enjoying. Not me, though. Champagne gives me a headache. It's not my thing. I'm not that girl.

Hank and the kids went down early and I agreed to meet them "soon" as I dodged the afternoon heat. I'd managed to delay it a while until our son, Allan's girlfriend, Anna, texted: "They've got Sonoma Cutrer!!!"

Then, Hank called. "Are you on your way?"

"I'm just leaving the house."

There is nothing flow-y or hip in my closet, so I settled for a pair of lightweight faded jeans and a loose blouse, threw on a necklace that might pass for cool, some hoop earrings and headed out.

Going by my neighbor Joanie's house, I called her and left a message. "Look outside, it's me walking down to the music festival. I know, shocking…"

After winding my way around the outlying golf course, I spotted Hank waving to me at the entrance. My mother's words played in my head…what would you do if you were dating him?

All around there were cute little food stands from LA restaurants. Craft Beer and Wine. Gift stands. All age groups were there milling about. Couples, foursomes, and families. "Look," I said, pointing to the miniature arch touting Arroyo Seco Weekend. "This is adorable!"

Music was playing at different set-ups, but it was the atmosphere I liked. It was fun. I was having fun.

We got what seemed a thimbleful of chardonnay for $18 and headed to where our kids were. I laid an old beach towel down and took a seat. Hilary offered me a lobster roll bathed in mayonnaise on fried bread. "This is so good," I said, savoring the richness of the food.

The music drew me in as I took another bite and sipped my drink.

At sixty, my children's mother had become that girl.

Cathy McArthur

Spinning the Racket

Words bounce in our heads
and over a net

on a court in the heat
mother and son—some space

across from us, a muse
motions to begin,

wants to play with us—
tennis, she says.

The nouns, the verbs pile up.
I've taught you this game

of sentences in the air,
one hit, then another.

You know a backswing,
a slice, a split step.

You and I take turns,
new rackets in our hands.

She's sweating,
we're cool, we're versed.

We talk; the phrases
gather in our court.

Venue, menu—
we tell her, *we're ready, just serve.*

LeConte Dill

Mama Has Dance Parties with Her 3-Year-Old Self

Sounds like there is a party in the background
Because there is
Usually 3000 miles between us
But tonight
Feels like just a living room
She say it might be Curtis Mayfield
one minute
then
Jaheim
the next
Ghetto Crooners
The Ghetto always
her home always has a song
She speaks in
1st person plural
"We groovin"
"That's our jam"
Her dance partner is
a 3-year-old middle child
big-eyed
and chocolate brown
her first words were cuss words
heard her parents screaming them
learned how to open the closet sliding door
and how to hide
in between
broughams and pocket books
Years later inherited that closet,
pocket book full of black & white photos,
cuss words
inherited a mortgage
and panic attacks
The 3-year-old taught the grown up to cock her head to the side
and smile for the camera
big-eyed
and chocolate brown
To groove to ghetto crooners
To find a song

Carol McMahon

Erie Canal: Another Early Morning Row

Small waves against the backs of oar blades
sound like wet cloth on a washboard.
What would Oma think
of this time spent on the water?
No lye soap, no wringer,
no taut line with clothespins like soldiers.

Up before dawn I'm sure she too saw
the moon on the wrong side of the day.
Those last hours wasted on sleep
could be transformed into a scrubbed floor,
flaky strudel or six sheets snapping.
She knew Opa would be pleased
by the work done. Anything less
would come at a price.

Pushing off from the dock
into spring's mist and new light
I anticipate only
geese, river otter, and the lone heron.
They, in turn, anticipate only
the water's flatness and the meal unawares.

At the day's end there is no fragrant pastry
or crisp sheet to justify the time spent.
No one to insist on an accounting.
Only this—in my mind's eye,
eddies circling outward
from the splash of fish and oar.

Judy Swann

In August in South Africa
        (A Blitz)

The U.S. men lost to Columbia
The U.S. men play Poland in August
In August the men will play Brazil
In August the women are not playing
Playing in August sucks anyway
And playing Brazil double sucks

Blitz is a team in Oklahoma and Syracuse
Blitz is a team in Hawaii and Virginia
In Virginia, the coach is Marlon LeBlanc
In Virginia, it is always too hot to play
Play if you must but bring your water
Play for Marlon, and play for mommy

Soccer moms ferry their young in convoys
Soccer moms' Volvos are not vulvas
Vulvas are not velvetty
Vulvas drip dry
Dry towels on the upholstery, please.
Dry up, meaning shut up is just as rude

Abby Wambach is thirty now!
Abby Wambach, the gold medallist from Rochester!
Rochester soccer cannot be poohpoohed
Rochester also has a couple good colleges
Colleges don't give many soccer scholarships
Colleges: how necessary are they?

Hope Solo is a kick-ass keeper
Hope Solo is a real person's name
Name me three soccer players
Name me one
One that I haven't named in this poem
One I don't know

Nenad Zigante played for the Wichita Wings
Nenad, whose friends call him Ziggy
Ziggy's wife Gretchen played for Japan
Ziggy's daughter was scouted by UNC
UNC also has good basketball
UNC is a division one school

Back to the Men's National Team
Back to Michael Bradley and Tim Howard
Howard is a hunka hunka burning
Howard did cry though, after South Africa
South Africa was too expensive for us to go to
South Africa's time will come

Maurice Edu's father is an immigrant
so Maurice Edu has an interesting name
Name me a Yankee, yeah a baseball player
Name the one who models for Canali
Mariano! Mariano Rivera! O. My. God.
Mariano Rivera is a fine, smokin' hot papi.

Papi.
God.

Cheryl Boyce-Taylor

YES

yes, she kissed me first
yes, I kissed her back
yes, our spirits flew
yes, I was married
yes, she was married too
yes, she smelled like apple blossoms
yes, earth said glory
yes, I held my breath
yes, she cried yes, yes
yes, she sang out loud
yes, she called me daddy
yes, the moon raised a brow
yes, the ocean came to see
yes, I heard the fiece beating of my heart
yes, there were hidden poems
yes, that was fucked up
yes, we could not stop
yes, I could not let go
yes, it went on for years
yes, someone got hurt
yes, I got no alimony
yes, we had regret
yes, I'd do it all again
yes, I should be filled with shame
but yes, I am not.

eve packer

sonnet for pure delight

oh it had been a terrible day
nutjob 2—henry bear where i did not buy large enuf gifts
for my grandkids then porter square books no outdoor play
but then, and then, my son picks us up and we speed to
foss park outdoor pool—45 minutes to go: its 6:
and in we jump and the world spins from hot & whiny—

the sun about to set, wide expanse of sky,
one older woman, 2 kids the only other ones in the swim,
& sam, my son, tosses my grandkids, jupiter & ozzy,
in the air, through the cool water, we are all splashing
and for a flash so fast a diamond prism far from
the maggots of hate and fear to this alternative
galaxy of pure wet play and delight

bliss

8.14.17: 7:19 pm

Donna J. Gelagotis Lee

Second Half

The women have gathered beneath
the umbrella pine,

their laps full of yarn, needles flashing
what sun is left as it drifts behind the islands

and into the sea, the sky pricked red.
Not one woman watches her hands

but, instead, each warms with a smile or
laughter as she tells tales of the day

and listens to what each will reveal.
The children play nearby,

and the men have all left for the
kafeníon. The sky is full of dusk.

The women brush off their skirts as
they rise and leave the empty chairs

facing one another in a half-circle
like a half moon one could swing on.

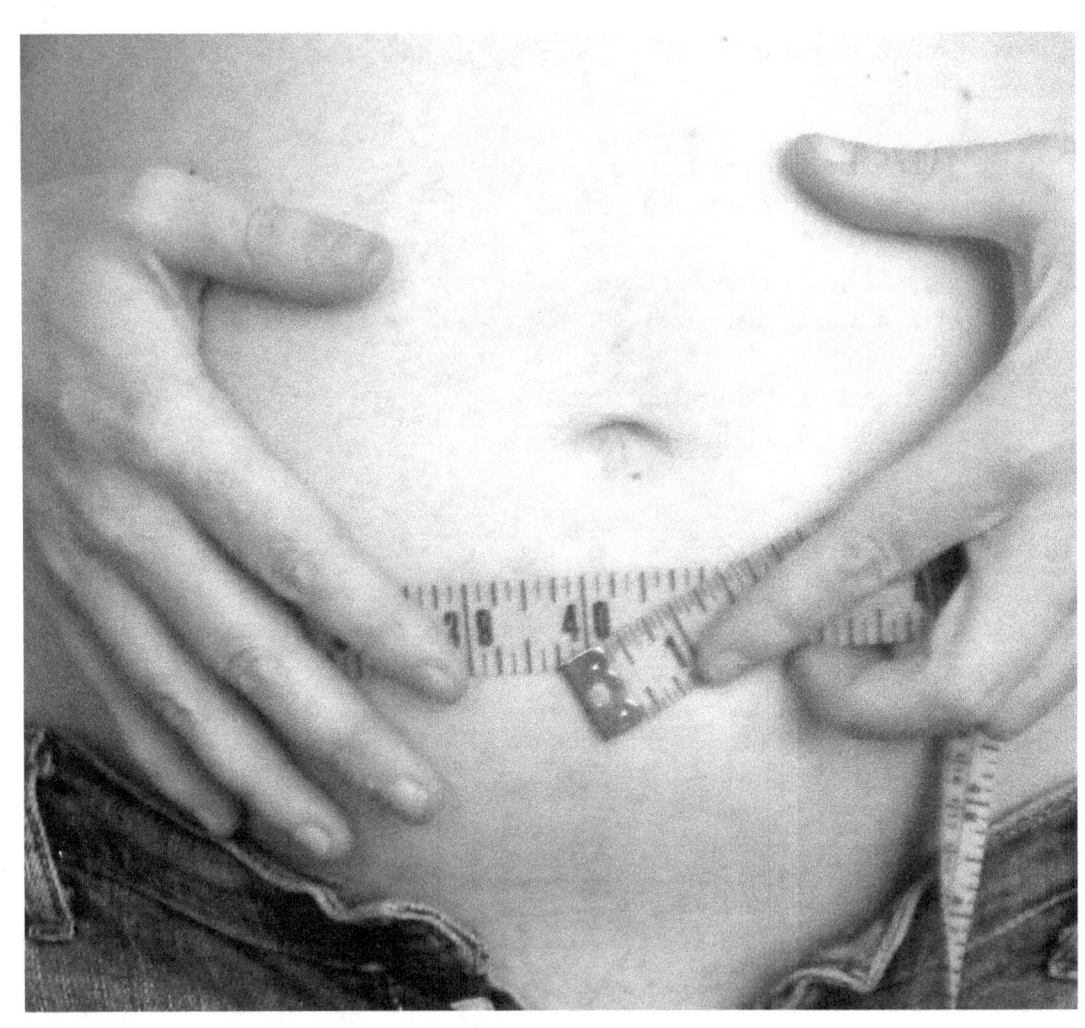

Heather Lewis

Faith Williams

You start these children

You start these children, little shoots,
half-unintended, carelessly, and then
they take over, like patches of wild mint,
making inroads on your lawn, a new
flavor, maybe bitter for you.
They're little machines, that you,
the sorcerer's apprentice, cranked up
and sent off on their way. Each fills
a room, a house, a life, and overlaps,
interpenetrates, steals, and fences off.
The Dead Kennedys and Gide,
the Miami Heat. Each runs around with your
unlived life. You don't mind their dirty socks
as much as yours, taken out of the back
closet and strewn across the landscape.
A pack of wild dogs, yes, but your heart rides
with them on their marauding raids.
And after they've gone, you look around
listlessly for new batteries, for the old shape
of the lawn. You hide out in hallways
and imagine enormous rooms.

Donna Katzin

On the Way Home

They share a chardonnay
at the French café on Broadway
—as busses belch, trucks backfire,
ambulances whine, and women shout
at overtired toddlers, ready
to call it a day.

The wine begins to do its work,
releases wrinkles between eyebrows,
unlocks a week's words shackled in their cells,
lightens losses, baggage of the heart.
Listening soothes wounds
like water over stones.

As darkness settles in, they return
to houses, husbands, kitchens,
kids to bathe, calls to answer,
one last memo for the office,
hunger for the wholeness
so easily broken.

Tami Haaland

Tell Me Something Isn't Coming

I dreamed I was making milk last night,
my breasts full, and I dripped some into a bowl
for relief. I didn't know what baby
caused this or where that child might be.
Years ago, one of my students spoke of her
mother, how old she was when this student
was born, and it was clear to her that such
a woman couldn't make milk. She looked
incredulous that I didn't understand,
but *here I am*, I thought, and *what did she know?*

It was so real, of course, in the usual way.
Sometimes I can't remember how it goes.
Only a few weeks ago I told someone
I had the good fortune to read Milton,
Paradise Lost, then *Regained.* I remember
the devils, but I can't place the conversation,
whether it was in recent travel, or local or
in a dream. But this I do know. Last winter,
a calm sea lapped at my bedroom window,
sun on the horizon. No reason to stay inside.

Jessica de Koninck

Fixing a Flat

Eating alone. I bought
a sandwich for dinner and wondered
how much of the cost was for labor,
how much of the cost was for product?

And on reflection realized
that all cost of product
is really cost of labor.

At lunch I had been talking
about negotiating with unions,
an improbable job for a poet
and labor sympathizer.

I spoke about the first time
my tire blew out on the highway.
I trusted coincidence.

The second time it happened
I began to remember
to park under the lights.

If only I could be consistent.
If only I could remember
component costs of labor.
If only I'd remembered
to park under the lights.

Maybe I wouldn't have kissed you.
Maybe my heart wouldn't
be punctured. I would not be
sitting here, eating alone.

Elizabeth Lara

Gemology

I dreamed my life a diamond, full faceted and far
from its mother mine. Around it I closed my fist,
warm palm against cold stone, lodestar
dreaming the life a diamond sees, full faceted and far.
How lucky to be a sister to the sun, no simple feldspar
under the cutter's tool, but fiery face of xenocryst.
I dreamed my life was a diamond. Full faceted. Far
from the mother mantle around it. Warming in my fist.

Laura Foley

After

After our three-hour bus ride to the city;
our seven hours marching in a crowd
of two hundred thousand;
after waving our signs:
Queer Grannies Against Trump,
till our arms ache
from repetitive motion's weight;
after our sumptuous dinner, with wine,
to celebrate our day of resistance,
we attend a three-hour play:
articulate screaming,
lewd gestures and sex,
an excess of passion
we grannies can only hope
to achieve through osmosis,
as we sleep in front row seats.

Carol Dorf

The Word "Future"

When I read the word *future* I notice
what a good scrabble word it would
be using up two u's like that.
Someone on Twitter wrote she was
praying the president wouldn't start a
war this weekend. I have lots of
plans, too. Conflicting political
events on Saturday and a play about
the Middle East on Sunday. I would
really like to see Sunday. I need to
write a calculus final before Monday.
Tonight M and her sons are coming
to dinner. We'll do a bit of Passover
— partially multicultural, partially
because their Jewish grandmother is
dead. My atheist mother-in-law
played a fierce game of scrabble,
reliably turned up at demonstrations.
I would like to pronounce the word
future with her confidence.

Devon Balwit

Small Dolmens

Early spring branches, still unleaved,
lift knobs to unknown singers. I mimic

badly with no response, yet for all that,
persist, awaiting the hot mouth

of my running dog, ball never dropped
at my feet, but elsewhere. Always,

I must work for what comes easily
to another. My imprint will be

hummingbird light, the world barely
quivering. Still, I labor. What else to do

with the sand as it spills, but mound it
in small dolmens, then celebrate

what I've made? Laugh if you like.
I'll mimic the over and undertones

scything before, the clarion ripple
that never quite shatters me.

CONTRIBUTORS' NOTES

Laura Ajayi is a mother-artist and educator based in Ottawa, Canada. Working primarily in textile and drawing media, her practice centers around issues of mothering and the maternal. Using the language of traditional women's work and of feminist visual culture, she examines the intersections of the erotically charged and the unremarkable, the familiar and the mysterious, the sexual and the nurturing.

E.J. Antonio is a recipient of fellowships from the Hurston/Wright Foundation, the Cave Canem Foundation and the New York Foundation for the Arts. She is the author of two chapbooks, *Every Child Knows,* (Premier Poets Chapbook Series 2007) and *Solstice,* (Red Glass Books, 2013), and a CD, "Rituals in the marrow: Recipe for a jam session." www.ejantoniobluez.net.

Cristin O'Keefe Aptowicz is the author of seven collections of poetry and two nonfiction books, most recently the New York Times bestselling *Dr Mütter's Marvels: A True Tale of Intrigue and Innovation at the Dawn of Modern Medicine.* Recent awards include an NEA Fellowship, the ArtsEDGE Writer-in-Residence position at the University of Pennsylvania, and the Amy Clampitt House Residency. Her seventh poetry book, *How to Love the Empty Air,* is forthcoming in March 2018. www.aptowicz.com.

Robyn Art is the author of *Farmer, Antagonist,* which was selected by Jennifer L. Knox as the winner of the 2015 Burnside Review Chapbook Contest and published in Spring 2016. Her full-length poetry collection, *The Stunt Double in Winter* (Dusie 2007) was a Finalist for the 2005 Sawtooth Poetry Prize as well as the 2005 Kore Press First Book Award. Her newer manuscript, *Amplitude, Awe,* was recently selected as a Finalist for the 2014 Burnside Review Book Award.

Devon Balwit teaches in Portland, OR. She has six chapbooks and two collections out or forthcoming, among them *We Are Procession, Seismograph* (Nixes Mate) and *Motes at Play in the Halls of Light* (Kelsay Books). Her individual poems can be found in *Cordite, The Cincinnati Review, The Carolina Quarterly, Fifth Wednesday, Red Earth Review, The Fourth River, The Free State Review, Rattle, The Inflectionist Review, Posit,* and more.

Nina Bannett's poetry has appeared in print journals such as B*ellevue Literary Review, CALYX, LUMINA,* and *WomenArts Quarterly,* and online at *Topology, the fem, Snapdragon,* and *Amygdala.* She has published a chapbook, *Lithium Witness,* and a full-length collection, *These Acts of Water* (ELJ Publications, 2015). She is Professor of English and department chairperson at New York City College of Technology, CUNY.

Cheryl Boyce-Taylor is the author of four collections of poetry. Her most recent, *ARRIVAL,* was published by TriQuarterly Books in June of 2017. A VONA Fellow, she has taught poetry workshops for: Cave Canem, New York Public Library, Poets & Writers, and UrbanWord NYC. Her poems have been published in *Poetry, Prairie Schooner, Killens Review of Arts & Letters* and in *Encyclopedia Vol. 3.*

Patrice Boyer Claeys is enjoying the freedom of the empty nest. She thanks her writing group, Plumb Line Poets, of Evanston, Illinois, for keeping her chiseling away. Her work has appeared in the *Mom Egg Review, Found Poetry Review, Blue Heron, Avocet, ARDOR, the Aurorean,* and *Bird's Thumb.* She was a featured artist in *Light, a Journal of Photography & Poetry.* Patrice reads for *MER* and was nominated for Best of the Net.

Susan Craig is a writer and semi-retired graphic artist living in South Carolina. She's passionate about issues of compassion, social justice, and ecology, all of which call her more deeply into the work of writing. Her poetry has been published or will appear in *Jasper Magazine* Fall 2018; *Fall Lines Literary Convergence,* 2017; *Kakalak* 2015 & 2016; Poetry *On The Comet,* public transit initiative by Columbia's poet laureate; chapbook *The Collective I*; and online journal *Quorum.*

Lorraine Currelley - Poet, writer, artist and healthy aging advocate. Widely anthologized awards recipient. Publications and honors include *Mom Egg Review, DoveTales, Belladonna, Blind Beggar Press,* and *Poets/Artists Magazine.* A recipient of an Arts For A Lifetime Grant by the New York Public Library, a Bronx Council for the Arts Su-Casa Residency, and Out of the Binders Scholarships. Recognized by the Association of Writers and Writing Programs and Poets & Writers. The executive director of Poets Network & Exchange and the Bronx Book Fair.

Nicelle Davis is a California poet, collaborator, and performance artist who walks the desert with her son J.J. in search of owl pellets and rattlesnake skins. Her poetry collections include *The Walled Wife* (Red Hen Press, 2016), *In the Circus of You* (Rose Metal Press, 2015), *Becoming Judas* (Red Hen Press, 2013), and *Circe* (Lowbrow Press, 2011). Her poetry film collaborations with Cheryl Gross have been shown across the world.

Jessica de Koninck is the author of one full-length collection, *Cutting Room*, and one chapbook, *Repairs*. A grandma, and a former attorney, she holds an M.F.A. from Stonecoast and a B.A. from Brandeis.

Penny Dearmin is both an Assistant Professor of English and Writing Center Director. Her work can be found in *Madcap Review* and *Vine Leaves Literary Journal*. Penny holds an M.F.A. from Georgia College as the recipient of the Flannery O'Connor scholarship. She's hard at work on her memoir, "Little Deaths," but her children are only interested in the wifi password.

Mary Di Lucia is the author of *Accompaniments*, a collection of stories inspired by photographs of St. Petersburg (Red Hook Editions, 2017). Throughout her life as a writer, she has collaborated with visual artists, most recently featured in *The Brooklyn Rail*. Mary teaches literature in the Bard Prison Initiative and is on the Language & Thinking faculty at Bard College.

Dr. LeConte Dill was born and raised in South Central Los Angeles, California and is currently creating a homeplace in Bed-Stuy, Brooklyn. She is a scholar, educator, and a poet in and out of classroom and community spaces, focusing on Blackgirl wellness. She holds degrees from Spelman College, UCLA, and UC Berkeley, has participated in VONA Voices and Cave Canem creative writing workshops, and was a 2016 Callaloo Creative Writing Workshop Fellow.

Alexa Doran is a mother, a lyrical gangster, and Ph.D student at FSU. She has recently been featured or is forthcoming in *CALYX, The Pinch, Guernica, The Dr. T.J. Eckleburg Review, Juked* and *Posit* literary magazines. Her poem "Emmy Hennings: Access is Excess" won first place in the 2016 Sidney Lanier Poetry competition, and her poem "Directions to My Body for the Uninitiated" was recently a finalist in the 6th Annual *Gigantic Sequins* Poetry Contest.

Carol Dorf has two chapbooks available, *Some Years Ask,* (Moria Press) and *Theory Headed Dragon,* (Finishing Line Press.) Her poetry appears in previous issues of *Mom Egg Review, Sin Fronteras, E-ratio, Great Weather For Media, About Place, Glint, Slipstream, Surreal Poetics, The Journal of Humanistic Mathematics, Scientific American*, and *Maintenant*. She has one daughter in college, is poetry editor of *Talking Writing*, and teaches math in Berkeley, CA.

Elizabeth Ehrlich is the author of *Miriam's Kitchen: A Memoir*, which won a National Jewish Book Award and was a New York Times Notable Book of the Year. Her poems have appeared recently in *Sugar House Review, WomanArts Quarterly, Muddy River Poetry Review, Pretty Owl Poetry, The Rondeau Roundup,* and *Tipton Poetry Journal*. She lives and works in New York.

Tara A. Elliott lives on the Eastern Shore of Maryland where she lives with her husband and son. She is the founder and director of Salisbury Poetry Week and is honored to have served as Wicomico County Public Library Light of Literacy Educator. Her recent poems have appeared in *The Ekphrastic Review, The TAOS Journal of International Poetry & Art,* and are forthcoming in *Three Drops from a Cauldron, Triggerfish Critical Review,* and *Wildness*.

Sara Epstein is a clinical psychologist from Winchester, Massachusetts, who writes poetry and songs, especially about light and dark places. Her poems recently appeared in *Third Wednesday, Chest Journal, Literary Mama, Women Outdoors Magazine, Wild Swans,* and two anthologies: *Sacred Waters*, and *Coming of Age*.

CLS Ferguson, Ph.D, speaks, signs, acts, publishes, sings, performs, writes, paints, teaches and rarely relaxes. Her collection *Soup Stories* is out on Portage Press. She and her husband, Rich are raising their daughter, Evelyn and their Bernese Mountain Border Collie Mutt, Sadie in Alhambra, CA.
http://clsferguson.wix.com/clsferguson

Laura Foley is the author of six poetry collections: most recently, *WTF* and *Night Ringing*. Her poem "Gratitude List" won the Common Good Books poetry contest and was read by Garrison Keillor on The Writer's Almanac. Her poem "Nine Ways of Looking at Light" won the Joe Gouveia Outermost Poetry Contest, judged by Marge Piercy. A palliative care volunteer in hospitals, she lives with her wife and their two dogs among the hills of Vermont.

Jen Stewart Fueston lives in Longmont, Colorado. Her work has appeared in a wide variety of journals and anthologies. The forthcoming poem, 'Trying to Conceive,' was a finalist for *Ruminate* magazine's McCabe poetry prize. Her chapbook, *Visitations*, was published in 2015. She has taught writing at the University of Colorado, Boulder, as well as internationally in Hungary, Turkey, and Lithuania.

Sherine Elise Gilmour graduated with an M.F.A. in Poetry from New York University. She has been nominated for a Pushcart Prize, and her poems have appeared or are forthcoming from *Green Mountains Review, Many Mountains Moving, Oxford University Press, River Styx, So To Speak, Tinderbox,* and other publications.

Tami Haaland is the author of two books of poetry: *When We Wake in the Night,* and *Breath in Every Room.* Her third volume, *What Does Not Return,* is forthcoming from Lost Horse Press in spring 2018. Her poems have recently appeared in *Ascent, Redheaded Stepchild, Consequence, South Dakota Review* and a variety of anthologies. They have been featured on The Writer's Almanac, Verse Daily, and American Life in Poetry. Haaland lives and teaches in Montana.

Heather Haldeman lives in Pasadena, California. She has been married to her husband, Hank, for thirty-eight years and has three grown children. Her work has been published in *The Christian Science Monitor, Chicken Soup for the Soul, From Freckles to Wrinkles, Mom Egg Review,* and numerous online journals. She has received first, second and third prizes for her essays. Currently, she is working on a memoir. Visit her blog at Heatherhaldeman.blogspot.com.

Lois Marie Harrod is the author of 16 poetry collections, most recently *Nightmares of the Minor Poet* (Five Oaks Press 2016). A Dodge poet and a three-time recipient of a NJ Council on the Arts Fellowship, she also writes short stories and teaches Creative Writing at the The College of New Jersey. Her work has appeared in journals and online ezines from *American Poetry Review* to *Zone 3.* Visit www.loismarieharrod.org for online links.

Tamara Hart is a Ukrainian-American poet and essayist whose work reflects her heritage, motherhood and the passage of time. Her writing has recently appeared in *The New Engagement, Driftwood Press, Lunch Ticket,* and *Nagatauk River Review,* among others. In 2016, her work was nominated for a Pushcart Prize. She lives and works as an English instructor in New Jersey with her sweet baby boy and two overfed cats.

John Oliver Hodges studied photography at the Southeast Center for Photographic Studies in Daytona Beach. His images have been collected in several books, including *Squares* and *Night Spiders.* He participated in Light Work's artist in residency program. His photos have been featured in *Juxtapoz Magazine, Hamburger Eyes, Ain't-Bad,* and many other venues. Additionally he has published three books of fiction. He currently lives in New Jersey, where he teaches writing.

Matt Hohner, a Baltimore native, holds an M.F.A. in Writing and Poetics from Naropa University in Boulder, Colorado. His work has been shortlisted for the Ballymaloe International Poetry Prize, awarded both third and first prizes in the Maryland Writers Association Poetry Prize, and won the 2016 Oberon Poetry Prize. His book-length manuscript, *Thresholds,* will be published by Apprentice House Press in Fall 2018. Hohner has work forthcoming in *Comstock Review.*

Tom Holmes is the editor of *Redactions: Poetry & Poetics* and the author of three full-length collections of poetry, most recently *The Cave* (winner of The Bitter Oleander Press Library of Poetry Book Award for 2013), as well as four chapbooks. His writings about wine, poetry book reviews, and poetry can be found at his blog, The Line Break: http://thelinebreak.wordpress.com/. Twitter: @TheLineBreak.

Jennifer Schomburg Kanke currently lives in Tallahassee, Florida, where she teaches creative writing and critical theory as a visiting professor at Florida State University. Her work has appeared in *Prairie Schooner, Court Green,* and *Fugue,* and she is the reviews editor for *Pleiades.*

Donna Katzin is executive director of Shared Interest, a social investment fund promoting equitable development in Southern Africa. She also coordinates Tipitapa Partners, working with organized women in Nicaragua, and serves on the board of the Center for Community Change. She is the proud mother of Sari and Daniel Altschuler, and author of *With These Hands* -- poems and photographs, available from Shared Interest (sandra@sharedinterest.org), inspired by South Africans in the struggle for economic justice.

Tina Kelley's third poetry collection, *Abloom & Awry*, came out in 2017 from CavanKerry Press, joining *Precise* and *The Gospel of Galore*, which won a 2003 Washington State Book Award. *Ardor* won the 2017 Jacar Press chapbook competition. A former *New York Times* reporter, she shared in a staff Pulitzer for 9/11 coverage and co-authored *Almost Home: Helping Kids Move from Homelessness to Hope*. She lives in New Jersey with her husband and two children.

Cheryl Klein is the author of *The Commuters* (City Works Press) and Lilac Mines (Manic D Press). She has been writing her way through parenthood in *MUTHA Magazine, Blunderbuss*, and on her blog at breadandbread. blogspot.com. She works at 826LA, a youth writing and tutoring center, and is completing a memoir about the many detours on her road to motherhood.

Deborah Kahan Kolb is a New York poet, dancer, and performer. Much of her poetry is informed by the unique experiences and challenges of growing up in, and ultimately leaving, the insular world of Hasidic Judaism. Her work has appeared in a number of print and online publications, and her debut poetry collection, *Windows and a Looking Glass* (Finishing Line Press 2017), was a finalist for the 2016 New Women's Voices Chapbook Competition.

Veronica Kornberg is a poet based in the town of Pescadero, on the Central Coast of California. Her poems have appeared or are forthcoming in *Tinderbox Poetry Journal, Valparaiso Poetry Review, Catamaran Literary Reader, Redactions: Poetry and Poetics, New Millennium Writings,* and *Negative Capability*. She is currently at work on her first book of poems.

Rebecca L'Bahy lives in central Massachusetts and currently works in the Boston area. She believes she holds the award for the longest time taken to complete an M.F.A. in creative writing--22 years! The proud mother of three children, her work has appeared in *Brain, Child, Writers Resist,* and elsewhere. "Ode to My Commute" is her first poem to appear in a print journal.

Jan LaPerle lives in east Tennessee with her husband, Clay Matthews, and daughter, Winnie. She has published a book of poetry, *It Would Be Quiet* (Prime Mincer Press, 2013), an e-chap of flash fiction, *Hush* (Sundress Publications, 2012), a story in verse, *A Pretty Place To Mourn* (BlazeVOX, 2014), and several other stories and poems. In 2014 she won an individual artist grant from the Tennessee Arts Commission.

Elizabeth Lara's poems have appeared in numerous online and print journals, including *Edna; Confluencia in the Valley; Truck; Ex Tempore; The Wide Shore: A Journal of Global Women's Poetry;* and *Nasty Women Poets: An Unapologetic Anthology of Subversive Verse*. In 2011 she was a resident at the Millay Colony. She co-edited *Happiness: The Delight-Tree – An Anthology of Contemporary International Poetry* (United Nations SRC Society of Writers, 2017).

Donna J. Gelagotis Lee is the author of *On the Altar of Greece*, winner of the Seventh Annual Gival Press Poetry Award and recipient of a 2007 Eric Hoffer Book Award: Notable for Art Category. Her poetry has appeared in numerous journals and anthologies, including *The Bitter Oleander, Feminist Studies, The Massachusetts Review, Mothers and Sons: Centering Mother Knowledge* (Demeter Press, 2016), and *Women's Studies Quarterly*.

Michael Levan has work in recent issues of *Arts & Letters, Painted Bride Quarterly, Iron Horse Literary Review, Copper Nickel, Ruminate,* and *Hunger Mountain*. He is an Assistant Professor of English at the University of Saint Francis and writes reviews for *American Microreviews* and *Interviews*. He lives in Fort Wayne, Indiana, with his wife, Molly, and children, Atticus, Dahlia, and Odette.

Heather Lewis completed a Master of Fine Arts degree from Savannah College of Art and Design, a Bachelor of Arts degree from East Carolina University, and an Associate in Arts from the Art Institute of Atlanta. She currently works at the University of North Carolina and takes creative writing courses at the Center for Documentary Studies.

Judith Lichtendorf is a mom (one perfect son), stepmom (four perfect women), and grandmother to two amazing delightful perfect children. She has studied fiction at the Ninety Second Street Y, Center For Fiction, and NY State's summer program in Saratoga Springs. Teachers include Lore Segal, Christopher Sorentino, Phillip Lopate, Rick Moody and Teddy Wayne, and life.

Tsaurah Litzky is a widely published writer of poetry, fiction erotica, memoir and commentary. Her major poetry collections are *Baby On The Water* (Long Shot Press) and *Cleaning The Duck* (Bowery Books). Her fifteenth poetry chapbook is *Full Lotus - Yoga Poems* (NightBallet Press). Just out from Unbearables/Autonomedia is her new memoir, *Flasher*. Tsaurah lives on the Brooklyn Waterfront where she sees the Statue of Liberty, icon of free women everywhere, from her kitchen window.

Poet, essayist and painter, Anne MacNaughton writes and teaches in New Mexico. Her work has been published in *The Notebook, The Best Poetry of 1989, Rag and Bone Shop of the Heart,* and *In Company: an Anthology of New Mexico Poets*. She co-founded and directed the Taos Poetry Circus, and was awarded the New Mexico Literary Association's Gratitude Award. She writes in an adobe cabin overlooking a mountain lake and canyon in a wildlife reserve.

Katie Manning is the founding Editor-in-Chief of Whale Road Review and an Associate Professor of Writing at Point Loma Nazarene University in San Diego. She is the author of *Tasty Other*, which won the 2016 Main Street Rag Poetry Book Award, and four chapbooks, including *The Gospel of the Bleeding Woman*. Her poems have appeared in *Fairy Tale Review, New Letters, Poet Lore, Verse Daily*, and many journals and anthologies. Find her online at www.katiemanningpoet.com.

Libby Maxey is a senior editor at the online journal *Literary Mama*, where she has been a part of the Literary Reflections department since 2012. She reviews poetry for *Mom Egg Review* and *Solstice*, and her own poems have appeared in *Mezzo Cammin, Crannóg, Kestrel, Naugatuck River Review*, and elsewhere. Her nonliterary activities include singing classical repertoire and mothering two sons.

Poetry and prose by Carole Mertz appear in *Arc Poetry, Copperfield, CutBank, Eclectica, Indiana Voice Journal, Mom Egg Review, Prairie Light Review, Society of Classical Poets, South 85 Journal, Voices de la Luna, WOW! Women on Writing, Working Writer, WLT, WPWT, 1888.center,* and in anthologies. *Writing After Retirement*, Smallwood and Redman-Waldeyer, Eds., (Rowman & Littlefield, 2014) includes her writing tips on good time management. Carole is the winner of several Wilda Morris Poetry Challenges. She resides with her husband in Parma, Ohio.

Cathy McArthur (aka Cathy Palermo's) poetry was recently published in *LIGHT, A Journal of Poetry and Photography*, and is forthcoming once again in the *Bellevue Literary Review*. Her work has previously appeared in the *Mom Egg Review* and also in *Juked, Barrow Street, Pilgrimage, Lumina, The Valparaiso Poetry Review*, and others. She lives in Queens, New York, and she teaches composition to medical students and also creative writing at The City College of New York.

Carol McMahon is a teacher and poet whose work has been published, or is forthcoming, in various journals (*IthacaLit, Prodigal, Clockhouse, Painted Bride Quarterly, Stone Canoe*) and has a chapbook, *On Any Given Day*, published by FootHills Press. McMahon received an M.F.A. in Poetry from the Rainier Writing Workshop and, when she is not with 11-year-olds, spends her time either running or rowing.

Gail Newman's poems have appeared or are forthcoming in journals and anthologies including *Canary, Prairie Schooner, Calyx, Hiram Poetry Review, Spillway, Naugatuck Poetry Review, Ghosts of the Holocaust, Prism, The Doll Collection, Feminist Poetics,* and *The Northern California Jewish Journal*. A collection of poetry, *One World*, was published by Moon Tide Press.

Rebecca Hart Olander's poetry has appeared recently in *Radar Poetry, Ilanot Review*, and *Yemassee Journal*, and her critical work has appeared in *Rain Taxi Review of Books, Solstice Literary Magazine*, and *Valparaiso Poetry Review*. She won the 2013 Women's National Book Association poetry contest, and her work has been nominated for a Pushcart Prize. Rebecca teaches writing at Westfield State University and is the editor/director of Perugia Press. You can find her at rebeccahartolander.com.

eve packer - Bronx-born, poet/performer/actress. Appearing widely with dance, poetry, performance, music, theatre. NEH, NYSCA, NYFA awards. Downtown Poet of the Year awards. Numerous publications. 3 poetry books (Fly by Night Press). 5 poetry/jazz CD's. Teaches at WCC. Mom, Grandmom, lives downtown, swims daily. (evebpacker@aol.com).

Laura Page is a poet and artist from the Pacific Northwest. Her work has appeared or is forthcoming in *Rust + Moth, Crab Creek Review, The Rumpus, Tinderbox Poetry Journal, TINGE,* and elsewhere. Her chapbook, *epithalamium,* was selected by Darren C. Demarree, as the winner of Sundress Publications chapbook contest, and is forthcoming. Laura is editor-in-chief of the poetry journal, *Virga.*

Mary Pan is a writer and family medicine physician with training in global health and narrative medicine. Her work has been published in several print and online publications including *Intima, Mothers Always Write, Pulse* and *Mamalode,* among others. She lives in Seattle with her husband and three young children. More at marypanwriter.com.

Preeti Parikh writes poems and essays in Ohio. Raised in India, she has a past educational background in medicine, and is presently a stay-at-home parent. Preeti's study of poetry has been supported by the AWP Writer to Writer Mentorship Program, Bread Loaf Writers' Conference, Stanford Continuing Studies, and other workshops. Her poems have been featured in or are forthcoming in *Literary Mama, For a Better World 2017, Cincinnati Walking Sonnet Project,* and *Cincinnati Poetry Month Daily.*

Kyle Potvin's chapbook, *Sound Travels on Water* (Finishing Line Press), won the 2014 Jean Pedrick Chapbook Award. She was a past finalist for the Howard Nemerov Sonnet Award. Her poems have appeared in *Bellevue Literary Review, Crab Creek Review, The New York Times, The Huffington Post, Measure, Mom Egg Review,* and others. She is an advisor to Frost Farm Poetry in Derry, NH, and helps produce the New Hampshire Poetry Festival.

Kristin Prevallet is a poet, performer, and educator. She is the author of five collections of poetry including *I, Afterlife: Essay In Mourning Time* (D'Un Devenir Fantôme) published in English by Essay Press and in French by Un bureau sur L'Atlantique; *Everywhere Here and in Brooklyn* was published by the Belladonna Collaborative. Aside from teaching for the Bard Prison Initiative, she is a hypnotherapist with a private practice in Westchester, NY. www.trancepoetics.com.

Tatiana Forero Puerta is originally from Bogotá, Colombia. Her work has appeared in *Able Muse, Literary Juice, Hawai'i Pacific Review, Juked,* and elsewhere. Tatiana is the author of *Yoga for a Wounded Heart* (Lantern, 2018) and a 2017 recipient of the Pushcart Prize. Her first poetry collection, *Cleaning the Ghost Room,* was a finalist in the Grayson Books Poetry Prize and Autumn House Prize for Poetry. Tatiana lives and teaches in NY.

Nancy Reddy is the author of *Double Jinx* (Milkweed Editions, 2015), a 2014 winner of the National Poetry Series, and *Acadiana* (Black Lawrence Press, 2018). Poems have appeared or are forthcoming in *Blackbird, The Iowa Review, Smartish Pace,* and elsewhere. The recipient of a Walter E. Dakin Fellowship from the Sewanee Writers' Conference and grants from the New Jersey State Council on the Arts and the Sustainable Arts Foundation, she teaches writing at Stockton University.

Catherine Rockwood lives near Boston, chasing a toddler, hunting for older kids' lost swim-goggles and particular treasured objects, and writing. Poems in *Antiphon, Literary Imagination, concīs, The Rise Up Review,* and elsewhere. Opinionated and occasionally salty essays and reviews in *Rain Taxi, Strange Horizons,* and *Tin House.*

Martha Joy Rose is a musician, community organizer, and museum founder. Her work has been published in blogs and academic journals. She is the NOW-NYC recipient of the Susan B. Anthony Award and founder of Mamapalooza. She created the Museum of Motherhood in 2003 and recently brought it to Historic Kenwood in St. Petersburg, Florida. MOM is devoted to the exploration of mother-labor and performance art. Upcoming publications include *Music of Motherhood* (2018) Demeter Press.

Margaret Rozga has published four books of poetry, including P*estiferous Questions: A Life in Poems* (Lit Fest Press, 2017). This book was written with the help of a Creative Writers Fellowship at the American Antiquarian Society. Her work has also appeared recently or is forthcoming in the *Whale Road Review, Peacock Journal,* and *Presence.* She writes monthly columns for *Milwaukee Neighborhood News* and for the *Los Angeles Art News.*

Hannah Baker Saltmarsh has been published in *The Kenyon Review, Feminist Studies, The Yale Review, The New Republic, Literary Mama,* and others. She lives in Hyattsville, Maryland with her husband and their two children.

Carol Seitchik comes to poetry after a long career in the visual arts. Her poems have been published in *A Feast of Cape Ann Poets* (Folly Cove Press), *The Endicott Review, Gemini Magazine, Mom Egg Review,* and other journals. She is also a Pushcart prize nominee. Seitchik lives with her husband in Beverly, Mass.

Margie Shaheed is a community poet, writer and teaching artist. Her work has appeared recently in *Mad River Review* and *Bookends Review*. She has four poetry chapbooks in print and is the author of *Tongue Shakers: Interviews and Narratives on Speaking Mother Tongue in a Multicultural Society* published by Hamilton Books, 2017.

Matthew Sharpe is the author of the novels *You Were Wrong, Jamestown, The Sleeping Father,* and *Nothing Is Terrible.* "Opera" is part of a series of short-shorts, some of which are posted at http://sharpestories.blogspot.com/.

Robin Silbergleid is the author of *Texas Girl* and *The Baby Book*. When she's not teaching or writing, you might find her puttering in her kitchen; her kids eat a lot of banana muffins.

Carissa Stevens is a high school English teacher and aspiring author. She lives in Berea, Kentucky, with her husband and dog. When she's not writing, she enjoys reading and reviewing young adult novels on her blog, I Read What They Read (ireadwhattheyread.com).

Marian Brown St. Onge retired six years ago from her position as founding Director of the Center for International Partnerships and Programs at Boston College, where she also taught French and directed BC's Women's Studies Program. Her publications include more than twenty poems and articles on women writers, cultural issues and topics in international education. Beyond her poetry, St. Onge is working on a biography of a World War II French Resistance fighter for which she received a Norman Mailer Fellowship award in 2009.

Judy Swann is an Ithacan and a project manager for a building performance/energy efficiency company. She is the editor of *We are all well: the letters of Nora Hall* (Young Bros, 2016). Her short story "Tell Me Her Name" won the Way to My Heart prize (2017). Her most recent poem is "Talking Elizabeth Cady Stanton" in *New York Votes for Women* (2017). She has Bob Dylan hair.

A high school English teacher, Katherine Barrett Swett lives in New York City with her husband and two sons. She received a Ph.D in American Literature from Columbia University. Her poems have been published or are forthcoming in various journals including, *The Lyric, Rattle, Mezzo Cammin, The Raintown Review* and *Measure.* Her chapbook, *Twenty-one* was published in 2016.

Elaine Terranova's seventh collection of poetry, *Perdido,* will be published by Grid Books. *Dollhouse* was winner of the Off the Grid Press 2013 Poetry Award. Her poems have appeared in *The New Yorker, The American Poetry Review, Women's Review of Books,* and other magazines, prose in *Boulevard, South Loop Review,* and *Hotel Amerika.* She has received a Pushcart Prize, a Pew Fellowship in the Arts, the Walt Whitman Award, and an NEA Fellowship in Literature.

J. C. Todd was awarded the Rita Dove Poetry Prize and holds fellowships from the Pew Foundation, Pennsylvania Council on the Arts, Ucross, Ragdale and others. Books include *FUBAR,* an artist-book collaboration (Lucia Press, 2016), *What Space This Body* (Wind Publications, 2008) and chapbooks, with poems in *APR, The Paris Review, Virginia Quarterly Review,* and most recently, *Beloit Poetry Journal* and *Canary.* She has taught poetry at Bryn Mawr College and the M.F.A. program at Rosemont.

Angela Narciso Torres's first book, *Blood Orange,* won the Willow Books Literature Award. Recent work appears in *Nimrod, Spoon River Poetry Review,* and *Water-Stone Review.* A graduate of Warren Wilson M.F.A. and Harvard Graduate School of Education, Angela has received fellowships from Bread Loaf Writers' Conference, Illinois Arts Council, and Ragdale Foundation. Born in Brooklyn and raised in Manila, she serves as a poetry editor for *RHINO* and a reader for New England Review. www.angelanarcisotorres.com

Meredith Trede's *Tenement Threnody* is from Main Street Rag Press (2016.) SFA State University Press published *Field Theory* (2011.) A Toadlily Press founder, her chapbook, *Out of the Book,* was in *Desire Path.* Other journal publications include *Barrow Street, Friends Journal, Gargoyle, The Paris Review.* She held fellowships at Blue Mountain Center, Ragdale, Saltonstall, VCCA, the Nicholson Political Poetry Award, and a NYFA travel grant. She serves on the Slapering Hol Press Advisory Committee. mtrede@meredithtrede.com.

Claudia Van Gerven has published in numerous journals, including *Mom Egg Review, Calyx, Prairie Schooner, The Georgetown Review,* and many others. She has won several national awards for her work. She is the author of four chapbooks, *The Ends of Sunbonnet Sue, Amazing Grace, Totem,* and *Bearing Witness.*

Jamie Wendt is a graduate of the University of Nebraska Omaha M.F.A. program. Her poetry has been published in various literary journals, including *Lilith, Raleigh Review, Minerva Rising, Blue Lyra Review,* and *Saranac Review.* Her essays on Jewish writing have been published in *Green Mountains Review* and the *Forward.* She contributes book reviews for the Jewish Book Council. Wendt teaches high school English and lives in Chicago with her husband and two children. https://jamiewendt.wordpress.com/.

A previous contributor to *MER,* Shanna Powlus Wheeler has published poetry in a wide range of print and online journals. Finishing Line Press published her chapbook, *Lo & Behold.* She recently completed a full-length poetry manuscript. A wife and mother of two, she directs the Writing Center at Lycoming College in Williamsport, PA.

Faith Williams lives in Washington, D.C. with husband and two dogs, was most recently a children's librarian in a charter school, and for years before that in other D.C. libraries, and before that taught English. She has been exchanging poems with a friend for a long time, almost 40 years. Her poems have appeared in *The Sow's Ear Poetry Review, Mom Egg Review, Poet Lore, Nimrod International, Kansas Quarterly, Tinderbox, Xanadu, Antiphon,* and *Comstock Review,* among others.

Sarah Anderson Wood is an adjunct professor at the University of Wisconsin-Madison teaching courses in American Literature. She received her Ph.D. in English Literature from the University of North Carolina. Wood is the mother of three children. Her poetry has been published in *Broad River Review* and *The Columbia Review.*

Margaret Young is the author of three poetry collections, *Willow from the Willow, Almond Town,* and *Blight Summer,* and the translator of Sergio Inestrosa's collection *El Espacio Improbable de un Haiku.* She lives in Beverly, Massachusetts, and teaches at Endicott College.

Dara Herman Zierlein's paintings touch topics such as equal & human rights, gender identity and environmental catastrophes. She has been interviewed with activists like Beth Terry, My Plastic Free life, *1 Million Women,* Australia, *Earth Issue* magazine in London, and in *Resist,* a tabloid edited by Francoise Mouly. When she is not painting, exhibiting, writing, teaching, working and submitting her art, she is at home in Mass. with her husband, son and five pets, peacefully enjoying the life of an artist.

MOM EGG REVIEW

Mom Egg Review Back Issues Available

Vol. 15		2017	Paper, 123 pp.	$18
Vol. 14	"Change"	2016	Paper, 128 pp.	$18
Vol. 13	"Compassionate Action"	2015	Paper, 154 pp.	$18
Vol. 12		2014	Paper, 150 pp.	$18
Vol. 11	"Mother Tongue"	2013	Paper, 125 pp.	$18
Vol. 10	"The Body"	2012	Paper, 120 pp.	$18
Vol. 9		2011	Paper, 120 pp.	$18
Vol. 8	"Lessons"	2010	Paper, 120 pp.	$18
Vol. 7		2009	Paper, 124 pp.	$18

*Plus US shipping $3.50 for the first book, $1.00 for each additional book.

Subscribe to *MER*

US shipping is free for subscription copies!

One year $18
Two years $36

Order on the web at
www.momeggreview.com (Click "Shop")

or mail your order with a check to

Mom Egg Review
Half-Shell Press
PO Box 9037
Bardonia, NY 10954

Contact: info@themomegg.com

Email info@themomegg.com for info about discounts for quantity purchases and for classroom use, or for out-of-country shipping.